the b

essential wedding

checklists

Sharon Naylor

SOURCEBOOKS, INC.®
NAPERVILLE, ILLINOIS

Published by Sourcebooks, Inc.
P.O. Box 4410, Naperville, Illinois 60567-4410
(630) 961-3900
FAX: (630) 961-2168
www.sourcebooks.com

Library of Congress Cataloging-in-Publication Data

Naylor, Sharon.
  The busy bride's essential wedding checklists / Sharon Naylor.
      p. cm.
  Includes index.
  ISBN 1-4022-0504-X (alk. paper)
  1. Weddings--Planning. I. Title.

HQ745.N3873 2005
395.2'2--dc22

2005016587

Printed and bound in Canada
WC 10 9 8 7 6 5 4 3 2 1

This book is dedicated to the memory and spirit of
Kate Reid.

CONTENTS

Appendix: Additional Worksheets

ACKNOWLEDGMENTS

- Deb Werksman is tops in my book as my dream editor at Sourcebooks.
- My agent Meredith Bernstein is always looking out for me, and for that I am incredibly grateful.
- Mike Napolitan—thank you for your fabulous work on my website! You are a genius and one of the most reliable people I've ever met.
- Scott Buhrmaster is a master of publicity, a fountain of wisdom, and the best guide any author could ask for.
- With thanks to my family and friends who have never let me down, and with thanks to my Mom, who follows every twist and turn of my work life and somehow keeps track of it all...even when she has bigger things to think about.

I'm lucky to have you all...

Introduction

Congratulations!

Right now, you've undoubtedly been hugged and toasted dozens of times. This is an amazingly bliss-ful time in your life...and you have a wedding to plan! This book will guide you and give you the #1 advantage in wedding planning: *organization*. Staying on top of things, knowing what needs to be done when, who's doing it, and who's paying for it is the best way to make the most of the planning months ahead. The details are outlined here, giving you an added boost of confidence and the security that you're not missing anything.

Nothing is ever perfect, but with this book it could be so streamlined a planning process as to almost seem that way.

That is my wish for you, and it is my inspiration in creating this checklist book for you both.

It's time now to get started on all the exciting tasks ahead...

Part One

Your First Steps

Making the Announcement

You've already called or emailed everyone you know with the news of your engagement, and your parents have shared the great news with everyone *they* know. They may even be planning an engagement party for you, complete with catering and lots of champagne. Everyone is just *thrilled!*

There's even more excitement to come, and even more people to make the announcement to.

To prepare for the exciting step of placing an engagement announcement in the newspaper, here's your checklist:

YOUR ENGAGEMENT PHOTO

___Plan to have your engagement photo taken by either a professional photographer you hire or a friend with an excellent digital camera.

___Choose the perfect setting for your engagement photo, such as on the beach, or in a garden.

___Set aside lots of time for the photo session.

___Plan what you'll both wear.

___Take several different shots, in several different

poses, to find the ideal choice.

___Have the photos developed, or upload them online to a site such as www.ofoto.com.

___Get a few printed in black and white if you wish.

___Get extra copies of prints and enlargements to keep and frame, and to share with friends and family.

CHOOSING YOUR NEWSPAPER

___Select which newspapers you'll submit your announcement to:

- · Your hometown paper(s)
- · Your parents' hometown paper
- · Your grandparents' hometown paper
- · The paper where you used to live and where many of your relatives and friends still reside

___Look in the paper (or on the paper's website) for their submission directions, such as what info to include and where to send your announcement.

___Send your engagement announcement in to the paper as soon as you'd like!

___Make sure you find out the date in which your announcement will appear, so that you can cut out your section as a keepsake.

___If it will be online, feel free to email the page link to your faraway friends and family.

YOUR WEDDING WEBSITE

A wonderful, twenty-first-century option for sharing the news of your engagement.

Check out www.wedstudio.com as an example of what can be done with today's unique wedding websites. Hint: this makes a great gift from parents to an engaged couple!

Here are some of the most popular options you might wish to add to your own site:

- ✓ The story of your engagement.
- ✓ The date, time, and location of your wedding— include links to the sites where your ceremony and reception will be held.
- ___ Links to your wedding registries.
- ___ Links to the hotels where guests can reserve their rooms, including the code for your block of rooms discount.
- ✓ Introductions to your wedding party, including pictures of them and short bios.
- ___ Pictures and short bios of your parents and grandparents.
- ___ Your wedding-weekend activities schedule, including who's hosting, what the event is, where to RSVP.
- ___ Babysitting contacts.
- ___ Links to any airline group discount plans, if your group will have to fly to your wedding location.
- ___ An online blog recounting the wedding plans as they're happening.
- ✓ An auto-countdown to your wedding date.
- ___ The results of guest polls and surveys.
- ✓ Detailed bios of both you and the groom, with

plenty of pictures of you both.

__Send everyone the announcement link.

Watch Out for Overkill!

It seems the trend just took off, and already the etiquette experts are complaining that some wedding websites are just *way* too loaded with details, rants, and over-the-top cheesiness. So consider that you can go too far in building your site. Keep the cute little childhood snapshots of you both to a minimum, and remember that what you put online is up for the entire world to see. Don't go too far!

Your wedding website's URL:

Your password:

(Write it here or keep it someplace secure and private)

Your "To Do" Timeline

You're off to a great start! Now, so that you have a grand overview of what you'll be doing month-by-month, here is a checklist of your general "to dos." You'll find more details in each category in the chapters to come.

Triple the Use of This Book!

Grab a few differently colored highlighter pens and highlight all those tasks that are yours to do, those your parents will take care of, the groom's parents' list, individual bridesmaids, the Maid of Honor, and so on. When you flip back to this list (and you will...often), you'll have a color-coded visual of what's still left to handle and who has it on his or her plate.

THE COUNTDOWN BEGINS...

One Year before the Wedding

__Announce your engagement.

__Place engagement photo and announcement in local newspapers.

__Attend engagement parties.

__Discuss with your parents and other planners

what your wishes are for the wedding.

___Meet with any family members who will participate in planning (or paying for) the wedding—this could be a casual dinner at your place.

___Begin looking through bridal magazines and wedding tips books for ideas.

___Talk to your recently married friends to get their vendor and site recommendations.

___Hire a wedding coordinator (optional).

✓Choose the wedding date and backup dates for site-booking coordination.

✓Inform your family and friends of the wedding date.

✓Create your wedding budget.

✓Decide who will pay for which elements of the wedding.

___Decide on your top budget priorities (i.e., which will get the most money—your gown, the caterer, flowers, photography, etc.).

___Request brochures for wedding vendor research, or visit experts' websites.

___Decide on your desired level of formality.

___Select the members of your wedding party and inform them of their roles.

✓Make up your own personal guest list.

✓Request guest lists from your parents and siblings.

___Create your final guest list, and get your final headcount for wedding size parameters.

✓Tour possible ceremony sites.

✓Select and book your ceremony location.

__Select and book your ceremony officiant.

__Discuss your ceremony plans with your officiant.

__Audition potential ceremony musicians.

__Hire your ceremony musicians and give them your play list.

✓Tour possible reception sites.

✓Select and book your reception site.

✗Research and book rental item agency, if necessary.

✗Create rental item needs list.

✗Visit with rental agency planner to look at their supplies, choose linen colors, china patterns, chair styles, etc.

✓Start shopping for your wedding gown.

__Order your wedding gown and veil.

__Start researching bridesmaid gown options.

__Collect bridesmaids' size cards and ordering information.

__Select and order bridesmaids' gowns.

__Start researching florists.

__Choose your florist and meet with the floral consultant to share your wishes.

__Research caterers and attend tastings.

__Select and book your caterer.

__Research cake bakers and attend tastings.

__Select and book your cake baker.

__Choose and book a photographer.

__Choose and book a videographer.

__Choose and book your reception entertainment: DJ, band, or musical performers.

___Choose and book a limousine or classic car company.

___Start looking at invitation samples, and select desired designs and wording.

___Notify your boss about your wedding date and arrange time off for the wedding and honeymoon week(s).

___Create your personalized wedding website.

All the Legalities

Don't forget to discuss the legal issues pertaining to your upcoming wedding, such as:

___Finding any previous relationship, divorce, or annulment papers the town will need to see before granting you a marriage license, or that your house of worship needs to see.

___Talking to an attorney about prenuptial agreements.

___Talking to an attorney about creating wills and other important documents.

___Talking to a financial advisor about your money goals.

Nine Months before the Wedding

___Find out your local marriage license requirements.

___Schedule the date you'll go together to apply for your marriage license.

___Schedule any medical tests necessary for your license to be granted.

___Meet with your officiant about your ceremony plans and pre-wedding classes.

___Meet with your caterer to discuss your menu, wedding setup, requirements, etc.

___Plan beverage requirements, bartenders needed, and bar setup.

___Select packages with your photographer.

___Select packages with your videographer.

___Select packages with your entertainers.

___Meet with your florist to design bouquets, boutonnieres, and floral décor.

___Meet with a travel agent to plan your honeymoon.

___Book your honeymoon.

___Apply for passports and travel visas if you will be attending an international destination wedding or honeymoon.

___Order your wedding invitations.

___Order your wedding programs.

___Order any additional printed items.

___Shop for and order your wedding rings.

___Have your wedding rings engraved (if applicable).

___Reserve all rental equipment (tents, chairs, etc.).

___Choose and reserve a block of rooms for your guests at the hotel.

___Book your honeymoon suite for the wedding night.

Six Months before the Wedding

___Choose and rent men's wedding wardrobe.

___Begin writing vows.

___Select ceremony music.

___Select ceremony readings.

___Register for wedding gifts.

___Send for name-change information, if necessary.

___Arrange for transportation for guests.

___Order pre-printed napkins, matchbooks, coasters, etc.

___Create maps to ceremony and reception locations for enclosure in the invitations.

___Start scouting for wedding photograph locations.

___Start planning the rehearsal dinner.

___Book rehearsal dinner site and caterer.

___Plan "wedding weekend" activities, such as brunches, sporting events, barbecues, children's events, tours, breakfasts, etc.

___Begin pre-wedding beauty treatments: skin care, massage, tanning, etc.

___If holding an at-home wedding, hire a landscaper to do lawn, trim shrubs, add extra plants or flowerbeds, mulch, etc.

___Make additional changes to home, such as painting rooms, installing carpet, etc.

Three Months before the Wedding

___Apply for your marriage license, according to the state's requirements.

___Go for your blood tests, according to the state's time requirements.

___Attend any premarital classes or counseling as required by your chosen faith.

___If summer, holiday, or destination wedding, send invitations to guests now.

___Assemble invitation packages with all inserts.

___Buy "Love" stamps at the post office.

___Begin your wedding gown fittings.

___Choose and purchase your shoes and accessories for wedding day.

___Bridesmaids' and mothers' fittings begin.

___Choose and purchase children's wedding day attire.

___Consult with your wedding coordinator for any updates, confirmations, or changes.

___Consult with caterer or banquet hall manager for updates.

___Ask honored relatives and friends to perform readings at the ceremony.

___Ask a relative or friend to serve as your emcee, and give him/her specific instructions.

___Practice your wedding vows!

___Finalize your selections of ceremony readings and music.

___Submit your song wish list to DJ or band, along with your list of spotlight dances.

___Submit picture wish list to photographer.

___Submit video wish list to videographer.

___Arrange for babysitters to watch guests' kids on the wedding day.

___Finalize and confirm plans for the rehearsal dinner.

Two Months before the Wedding

___Wedding gown fittings continue.

___Purchase your "going away" outfit and honeymoon clothes.

___Address invitations to guests (for non-holiday, summer, or destination weddings).

___Assemble invitation packages.

___Buy "Love" stamps at the post office.

___Mail invitations to guests six to eight weeks prior to the wedding.

___Order or make your wedding programs.

___Order or make your wedding favors.

___Meet with ceremony musician about song list.

___Have attendants' shoes dyed in one dye lot.

___Ask friends to participate in wedding, such as attending the guest book, transporting wedding gifts from reception to home, etc.

___Send for all name-change documents, such as passport, credit cards, driver's license, etc.

One Month before the Wedding

___Meet with officiant to get the final information on ceremony elements, location rules, etc.

___Invite officiant to rehearsal dinner.

___Plan the rehearsal.

___Invite wedding party and involved guests to the rehearsal and rehearsal dinner.

___Confirm honeymoon plans.

___Confirm wedding-night hotel reservations.

___Get all incoming guests' arrival times at airports and train stations.

___Arrange for transportation of guests to their hotel.

___Arrange for transportation needs of guests throughout the wedding weekend.

___Make beauty appointment for wedding day.

___Visit your hairstylist to "practice" with hairstyles for the big day.

___Visit your makeup artist for a practice run.

___Get pre-wedding haircut, dye, or highlights.

___Fittings for your dress continue.

___Pick up your wedding bands.

___Have your rings appraised and insured.

___Attend bridal showers.

___Send thank yous for bridal shower gifts.

___Call wedding guests who have not RSVP'd to get the final headcount.

___Create your seating chart for reception.

___Write up seating place cards and table numbers.

___Pick up honeymoon travel tickets and information books.

___Make up welcome gift baskets for guests.

___Purchase gifts for family members and wedding party.

___Wrap and label gifts.

___Purchase unity candle.

___Purchase garters (get two—one for keeping, one for tossing).

___Purchase toasting flutes.

___Purchase cake knife.

___Purchase guestbook.

___Purchase post-wedding toss-its (birdseed, flower petals, bubbles, bells, etc.) and decorate, or personalize, small containers, if you so choose.

___Purchase throwaway wedding cameras.

___Work on any do-it-yourself crafts you'll make for the wedding.

One Week before the Wedding

___Confirm all wedding plans with all wedding vendors:
  - Caterer (give final headcount now!)
  - Florist (give delivery instructions now!)
  - Cake baker
  - Photographer
  - Videographer
  - Lighting technician
  - Ceremony musicians
  - Reception entertainers
  - Officiant
  - Ceremony site manager
  - Reception site manager
  - Wedding coordinator
  - Limousine company (give directions now!)
  - Rental company agent

___Pay final deposits for all services.

___Place tips and fees in marked envelopes for such participants as the officiant, ceremony musicians, valets, etc.

___If supplying your own beverages, conduct a shopping trip to the local discount liquor and beverage supply house for stocking up.

___Visit a warehouse superstore to stock up on any items you'll need for the wedding weekend

(supplies to have at home, barbecue food, snacks, etc.)

___Drop off guest welcome baskets at hotel.

___Groom picks up tux.

___Groom and ushers pick up tux accessories, socks, shoes, etc.

___Arrange for house- and pet-sitters.

___Notify the local police department of your upcoming absence, so that they can patrol your neighborhood.

___Get travelers' checks (if you so choose).

___Plan wedding day brunch, and inform wedding party and guests about it.

___Plan your special toasts.

___Ready wedding announcements to be mailed the day after the wedding.

___Attend bachelor and bachelorette parties.

The Day before the Wedding

___Supervise delivery of rental items to wedding location.

___Supervise setup of all items at wedding location.

___Finish packing suitcases and carry-ons for wedding night and honeymoon.

___Stock your bag with your car keys, house keys, passports, ID's, marriage license, wedding night and honeymoon hotel confirmations, medications, ATM card, etc.

___Arrange to have your car, with your honeymoon suitcases in the trunk, left securely in the wedding night hotel's parking lot for use the next day.

___Lay out all wedding day wardrobe and accessories.

___Very important: plan your shower-time schedule for the next day!

___Hand out printed directions to all family members and wedding party members.

___Confirm times for all attendants to show up on the wedding day, and where to go.

___Arrange for someone to be in charge of handing out payment envelopes.

___Hit the ATM to get cash on hand for emergencies, tips, valet, etc.

___Assemble your emergency bag with extra stockings, lipstick, pressed powder, emery boards, etc.

___Put a cell phone in the emergency bag.

___Gas up the cars, just in case.

___Go to the beauty salon to get waxed and tweezed.

___Stock up on supplies for the wedding-morning breakfast, or call in your catering order.

___Place last call to caterer or coordinator to finalize plans.

___Attend the rehearsal and rehearsal dinner.

___Get a good night's sleep!

On the Wedding Day

___Set out favors and place cards at reception site, if manager will not be doing it.

___Set out post-wedding toss-its where appropriate at ceremony site.

___Set out guest book and pen.

___Attend bridal breakfast.

___Have a wedding day breakfast sent to where the men are getting ready.

___Have hair and nails done at beauty salon.

___Have makeup done.

___Be dressed early!

___Have photos taken at home.

___Double-check that someone responsible has arranged for your honeymoon suitcases to get into your car or to your hotel room.

___Double-check that the appropriate people have the wedding rings for transport to the ceremony.

___Make sure the bag with your car keys, house keys, ID's, passports, etc. comes with you to the wedding.

___Relax as you leave for the wedding!

___Attend the wedding.

___Have the time of your life!

___Attend the after-party.

___Have a safe ride home!

The Day after the Wedding—Chores to Assign

___Have someone supervise the return of rental company items.

___Have someone supervise clean-up of the site, if necessary.

___Get a signed receipt for the return of all rented items.

___Have tuxes returned to rental store.

___Hold day-after breakfast for guests.

___Transport guests to airports, train stations, etc. for their rides home.

___Hire cleaning service if your home was the site of the wedding festivities.

3

Creating Your Team

Here are the usual players in any wedding's team.
Check off those that you'd like to invite to be a part
of your wedding planning Inner Circle:

The Bride's Side
- ✓ Mother of the Bride
- __ Stepmother of the Bride
- __ Father of the Bride
- __ Stepfather of the Bride
- ✓ Maid/Matron of Honor
- __ Bridesmaids
- __ Flower girl
- __ Junior Bridesmaid

Other Players
- __ Grandparents
- __ Godparents
- __ Guardians
- __ Adoptive parents
- __ Siblings not in the wedding party

- __ Siblings' spouses or partners not in the bridal party
- ✓ Friends not in the bridal party
- __ And of course...the wedding coordinator

The Groom's Side
- __ Mother of the Groom
- __ Stepmother of the Groom
- __ Father of the Groom
- __ Stepfather of the Groom
- __ Best Man
- __ Ushers/Groomsmen
- __ Ringbearer

Here's where you'll name your Inner Circle and find out the basics of just what their roles and responsibilities are. You'll add your own tasks to their lists as the process goes along.

Maid/Matron of Honor

  Name: Jamie Kline

  Name:

(Yes, there are *two* spots here—some brides want to choose two, or have a Maid *and* a Matron of Honor. It could be a sister and a best friend, two sisters, two friends, a sister and your mother…You don't have to pick just one!)

___Offer to help the bride with any pre-wedding research or planning.

___Help the bride select the gowns for her and for the bridesmaids.

___Organize the bridesmaids' dress shopping trip.

___Collect the bridesmaids' size cards and payments for their gowns, shoes, and accessories.

___Pick up dresses for the bridesmaids (and if necessary mail via insured and tracked mail).

___Organize and attend fittings for dresses.

___Make your travel and lodging plans for the wedding weekend, and for any other times when you'll need to be present for the bride.

___Plan and host (or cohost) a shower for the bride.

___Inform guests about where the bride is registered.

___Attend all pre-wedding parties and events.

___Keep a record of gifts received by the bride at the shower and at pre-wedding parties.

___Coordinate all out-of-state bridesmaids' information, travel, and lodging plans.

___Inform the bridesmaids of the rehearsal and rehearsal dinner plans, and coordinate their transportation.

___Team up with the bridesmaids to purchase a shower gift and a wedding gift. You all may choose to give individual gifts rather than a group gift.

___Set up the appointment for the bridesmaids to get their hair, makeup, and nails done; organize the bridesmaids' trip to the salon.

___Confirm bridesmaids' on-time arrival on the day of the wedding.

___Provide stress-relief and comfort for the bride during the planning process—she'll need this service from you often!

___Help plan and attend the bachelorette party.

___Attend the rehearsal and rehearsal dinner; propose a toast to the bride and groom.

___Arrive early on the wedding morning to help the bride prepare.

___Help the bride get into her wedding gown and fasten her veil.

___Hold the groom's wedding ring for the ceremony.

___Arrange the bride's veil, train, and gown before the ceremony begins and wish her luck.

___Stand next to the bride during the ceremony,

and hold her bouquet during the vows. Hand over the groom's ring when the time is right.

___Help arrange the bride's train when she has to sit, stand, move, or walk as part of the wedding ceremony.

___Sign the marriage license as an official witness after the ceremony.

___Stand in the receiving line (your position is next to the groom).

___Play hostess during the receiving line, in case you have to introduce someone to the groom, and during the cocktail hour and reception. You facilitate mingling.

___Pose for post wedding pictures.

___Participate in special first dances, like your first dance with the Best Man.

___Propose a toast to the couple after the Best Man's toast.

___Bring reception guests onto the dance floor.

___Attend to the bride's needs during the reception.

___Attend to the needs of the bride's parents, if necessary.

___Be the go-to girl, for any problems that might arise during the reception.

___Help close down the party by leading guests out, collecting throwaway cameras, helping to bring the couple's gifts out to the car, arranging for safe rides home for guests.

___Attend the after-party.

___Help the bride prepare for and make her departure.

___Thank the wedding's hosts for a wonderful time.

___Attend the morning-after brunch or breakfast.

___Take care of the couple's home or pets while they're away on their honeymoon.

___Arrange to have any pictures from the wedding developed. If possible, arrange to have them left in the couple's room for their return.

___Optional: Plan a welcome home party for the couple.

Bridesmaids

Name: Heidi Hill

Name: Amy Cooper

Name:

Name:

Name:

Name:

Name:

Name:

___Offer to help the bride and groom with any pre-wedding tasks, such as scouting out locations, addressing envelopes, making favors, etc.

___Help choose the bridesmaids' dresses, shoes, and accessories. If at a distance, respond with your sizes in a timely manner.

___Make your own travel and lodging plans for the wedding weekend, and inform the Maid of Honor.

___Pay for your dress, shoes, and accessories.

___Select and wrap a shower gift, or pitch in for a group gift for the couple.

the busy bride's essential wedding checklists

___Plan, attend, and help host the bridal shower.

___Provide the bride with levity and comfort during the planning months while she's stressed-out.

___Pick up your dress and have it fitted.

___Attend all pre-wedding parties and events.

___Help plan and attend the bachelorette party.

___Attend the rehearsal, ready to learn.

___Attend the rehearsal dinner.

___Shop for and wrap a wedding gift for the couple, or pitch in on a group gift.

___Arrive on time at the bride's house on the day of the wedding.

___Attend the pre-wedding beauty salon trip, and have your hair, nails, and makeup done.

___Pose for pictures before and after the wedding.

___Be ready to depart on time for the ceremony.

___Stand in line as part of the wedding ceremony, and the receiving line after the ceremony has ended.

___Play hostess at the cocktail hour and during the reception, facilitating guest mingling, bringing guests onto the dance floor, and participating in any special spotlight dances.

___Be available to help with any needs the bride and groom have during the night.

___Help close down the party by escorting guests out, getting them safe rides home, helping to bring the couples' gifts out to the car.

___Attend the after-party.

___Attend any morning-after brunches.

___Be available to help with any cleanup or rental returns.

___Help plan a welcome home party for the couple, or take care of any remaining responsibilities while the bride and groom are away.

Junior Bridesmaid

Name:

___Attend any pre-wedding parties, bridal showers and the rehearsal and rehearsal dinner.

___Attend a dress-shopping trip to get your dress, shoes, and accessories—your dress will be similar (if not matching) to the bridesmaids' dresses.

___Attend the bridal shower.

___Give shower and wedding gifts to the couple.

___Arrive on time the morning of the wedding.

___Dress and prepare for the wedding.

___Pose for pictures before and after the wedding.

___Hand out wedding programs or packets of bird-seed to guests.

___Participate in the wedding ceremony.

___Stand in the receiving line.

___Participate in special dances during the reception.

___Attend the morning-after brunch.

Flower Girl

Name:

Name:

___Attend all pre-wedding parties.

___Shop with the bride and her parents for her

wedding dress, shoes, and accessories.

__If necessary, attend dress fittings.

__Attend the bridal shower, and give a gift.

__Attend the rehearsal, learn the role, and attend the rehearsal dinner.

__Give a wedding gift to the bride and groom, if not included in the bridesmaids' group gift.

__Arrive on time the morning of the wedding.

__Dress and prepare for the day.

__Pose for pictures before and after the wedding.

__Participate in the ceremony, sprinkling flower petals down the aisle during the processional.

__Participate in the receiving line.

__Participate in any special dances during the ceremony.

__Attend any morning-after wedding events.

The Best Man

Name:

Name:

(Again, there can be two!)

__Attend all pre-wedding parties.

__Volunteer to help the groom with any wedding-planning tasks.

__Help the groom search for, select, and rent wedding-day tuxedos and accessories for the men.

__Coordinate the men's tuxedo shopping and fitting expedition and the groomsmen's sending of their size cards and payments.

__Schedule the date and time the men will pick up their tuxes.

__Make your travel and lodging plans for the wedding weekend and help others in the wedding party do the same.

__Plan and host the bachelor party.

__Attend any wedding weekend events.

__Volunteer to help transport any incoming guests to and from the airport or train station.

__Attend the rehearsal and rehearsal dinner; learn your roles for the ceremony.

__Coordinate the group wedding gift from all the men, or select and wrap your own gift.

__Be there to counsel the groom whenever he needs to talk, or when he needs comic relief.

__Arrive on time on the wedding day, with all of your gear in tow.

__Pose for pictures before and after the wedding.

__Hang onto the wedding ring and make sure you have it in safekeeping at the ceremony.

__Stand next to the groom during the ceremony.

__Hand over the ring when the time comes.

__Sign the marriage license as one of the witnesses after the ceremony is complete.

__Pay the officiant's fee after the ceremony is over (you may be given a payment in an envelope for this by the groom or by one of the parents).

__Dance during spotlight dances at the start of the reception.

__Propose a toast at the start of the reception.

___Be a good host and facilitate mingling and danc-
ing during the reception.

___Help with cleanup, gift transport, and getting
the bride and groom to their hotel with their
luggage after the reception.

___Attend the after-party and attend the morning-
after breakfast or brunch.

___Collect all the men's rented tuxedos, shoes, and
other accessories for return to the rental agency.

___Help the couple's parents with any post-wedding
tasks, like the return of rented items.

Ushers and Groomsmen

Name:

Name:

Name:

Name:

Name:

Name:

Name:

Name:

___Attend any pre-wedding parties.

___Attend the tuxedo-shopping expedition and
make your payments.

___If you're at a distance, get your measurements
taken professionally and send them in to the Best
Man for your tuxedo rental.

___Make your travel and lodging plans for the
wedding weekend.

___Shop for your shoes and any other accessories you've been instructed to get.

___Help plan and host the bachelor party.

___Join in on decorating the getaway car.

___Pitch in on the couple's wedding gift, or purchase and wrap your own for them.

___Attend the rehearsal, rehearsal dinner, and learn your roles for during the ceremony—how to seat people, etc.

___On the wedding morning arrive on time with all of your gear in tow.

___Perhaps join the groom and Best Man for breakfast or a round of golf before it's time to get ready.

___At the ceremony, escort guests to their seats.

___Hand out wedding programs.

___Stand in line with the wedding party during the ceremony.

___Walk back down the aisle with the bridesmaid you're escorting.

___Pose for pictures before and after the wedding.

___At the reception, participate in any spotlight dances at the start of the party.

___Mingle, dance, and facilitate a great time for guests.

___Bring that decorated car around for the couple.

___Help with post-reception cleanup and transport of the couple's gifts.

___Attend the after-party and attend the morning-after breakfast or brunch.

___Return your tuxedo and any other rented items to the Best Man before you take off.

Ringbearer

Name:

Name:

___Attend any pre-wedding parties, with parents.

___Go on a shopping trip to select your wedding day wardrobe and accessories OR go with the men to be fitted for a tuxedo.

___Attend the rehearsal, learn the role, and attend the rehearsal dinner.

___Give a wedding gift to the bride and groom, if not included in the groomsmen's group gift.

___Arrive on time the morning of the wedding.

___Dress and prepare for the day.

___Pose for pictures before and after the wedding.

___Participate in the ceremony.

___Participate in the receiving line.

___Participate in any spotlight dances during the ceremony.

___Attend any morning-after wedding events.

Parents of the Bride and Groom

Bride's mother:

Bride's stepmother:

Bride's father:

Bride's stepfather:

Groom's mother:

Groom's stepmother:

Groom's father:

Groom's stepfather:

Others:

___Host any engagement parties or celebrations.

___Meet with the rest of the team, or the other set of parents, along with the bride and groom for a planning session.

___Decide who will help plan and pay for which parts of the wedding.

___Attend all pre-wedding parties, showers, etc.

___Make your travel and lodging plans for the wedding weekend.

___Select and purchase or rent your wedding day wardrobe and accessories.

___Choose a wedding gift for the couple.

___Attend the rehearsal and rehearsal dinner.

___Attend the bridal salon trip for hair, nails, and makeup (if applicable).

___Mothers: Be escorted down the aisle to your seat OR escort the bride and groom during the processional.

___Father of the bride: Escort the bride (possibly in tandem with her mother) down the aisle.

___Stand in the receiving line after the ceremony.

___Pose for pictures before and after the wedding.

___Participate in any spotlight dances at the start of the reception.

___Give a toast after the Best Man and Maid of Honor's toasts.

___Be great hosts and facilitate mingling and dancing.

__Take care of unforeseen dilemmas and requests during the event.

__Help with the party close down and clean up, and help transport the couple's gifts to their car or home.

__Take care of last-minute payments and tipping.

__Attend the after-party and attend the morning-after wedding breakfast or brunch.

__Help guests with their returns home.

__Take care of any remaining post-wedding tasks.

> The bride and groom's tasks are outlined within this book, so read on...

AND THE OTHERS...

Of course, there may be many additional people who play important roles in your wedding. They may not be in the wedding party, but they're honored participants nonetheless. Ask your closest friends and loved ones to play a role with the following:

__Standing at the ceremony entrance as an official welcome greeter.

✓ Perform a reading or song during the ceremony.

__Participate in any religious or cultural rituals during the ceremony.

__Stand at the ceremony exit to hand out directions to the reception and the hotel, or birdseed packets/bubble bottles.

__Hand out birdseed packets or bubble bottles.

__Pull the cord that releases the doves or butterflies.

___Ring the church's bells upon your exit.

___Propose a toast during the reception.

___Read messages from absent guests during the reception.

___Act as emcee during the reception. (More on the emcee's role in later chapters.)

___Propose a tribute to departed family and friends during the reception.

And other tasks you have in mind listed here:

-
-
-
-
-
-

The names and roles of these honored attendants are:

- Micah Bolander (Reading)
-
-
-
-
-
-
-
-

YOUR WEDDING COORDINATOR

You might wish to bring in an expert to help you with your wedding plans. After all, you're very busy, and the assistance from an in-the-know pro could help bring your wedding dreams to life. Use this checklist to see if you'd like help in any of the following areas, which can be booked as part of an all-inclusive package or individually as separate services:

___Finding the ceremony and reception sites.

___Finding reputable wedding professionals.

___Finding wedding professionals who are available on your wedding date.

___Helping you create the theme for your dream wedding.

___Helping you locate hard-to-find services or rental items.

___Helping with wedding coordinators' legal contracts.

___Helping with selecting rental items.

___Helping to facilitate a smooth working partnership between members of your team (i.e., mediating).

___Helping with setting up the site on the wedding day.

___Helping with directing wedding experts on the wedding day.

___Running the timing of all wedding-day events like clockwork.

___Troubleshooting anything that might go wrong on the wedding day.

___Coming up with quick solutions to save the wedding day.

___Overseeing cleanup and the return of rental items on the wedding day, so that you don't have to worry about it.

Your Wedding Coordinator Comparison Checklist

(Use this checklist to keep careful notes during your interview process in order to select the ideal wedding coordinator)

Wedding Coordinator #1:

Name:

Company name:

Address:

Phone:

Fax:

Email:

Website:

Cell phone number:

Days and hours of operation:

Ideal package includes:

Number of hours:

Overtime fees:

Payment plan:

Cancellation plan:

Years of experience:
Notes on skill and demeanor:
Dates of meetings with officiant:

Wedding Coordinator #2:
Name:
Company name:
Address:
Phone:
Fax:
Email:
Website:
Cell phone number:
Days and hours of operation:

Ideal package includes:

Number of hours:
Overtime fees:
Payment plan:

Cancellation plan:

Years of experience:

Notes on skill and demeanor:

Dates of meetings with officiant:

Wedding Coordinator #3:

Name:

Company name:

Address:

Phone:

Fax:

Email:

Website:

Cell phone number:

Days and hours of operation:

Ideal package includes:

Number of hours:

Overtime fees:

the busy bride's essential wedding checklists

Payment plan:
Cancellation plan:
Years of experience:
Notes on skill and demeanor:
Dates of meetings with officiant:

The wedding coordinator you've chosen is:
The date you signed the contract:
Here is where you'll keep a record of your appointments:

Wedding Coordinator Appointment Sheet:
Meeting date:
Time:
Location:
Length of meeting:
To discuss:

Meeting date:
Time:
Location:
Length of meeting:
To discuss:

Meeting date:
Time:
Location:
Length of meeting:
To discuss:

Meeting date:
Time:
Location:
Length of meeting:
To discuss:

Meeting date:
Time:
Location:
Length of meeting:
To discuss:

Meeting date:
Time:
Location:
Length of meeting:
To discuss:

the busy bride's essential wedding checklists

4

Creating Your Guest List

How do you keep your list under control? Create a priority list. I know it sounds harsh, but it's often the best way to create a realistic guest list that meets your needs of sharing the day with your own most important people:

Tier 1: Parents, siblings, grandparents, the wedding party and their guests, your best friends.

Tier 2: Aunts, uncles, cousins, good friends, and good work friends.

Tier 3: Distant relatives you haven't seen in a while but feel an obligation to invite, friends you haven't seen in a while but would like to reconnect with.

Tier 4: Work associates, colleagues, bosses, close neighbors.

Tier 5: Your parents' friends, siblings' friends, and others you could invite but don't have to.

Tier 6: Distant friends and family members you're being pressured to invite but could live without.

You might find that assigning tiers to your list will allow you to eliminate tier five and tier six, comfortably fitting your most desired guests into a more comfortable budget for you.

Collecting the Lists

To be sure you're organized, make sure you receive the following wish lists in time to create your master guest list, which will give you the magic number to set your wedding plans:

- ☑ Your list
- ☐ The groom's list
- ☑ Your parents' list
- ☐ The groom's parents' list
- ☐ Your siblings' lists

KIDS AND "AND GUEST"

Of course, there are always extra names that pop up during your list consideration process.

- Every single guest over the age of eighteen, for instance, should be given the option to bring a date to your wedding. No exceptions. It would be an insult *not* to give them the opportunity. So be prepared for some "slots" on your guest list to be filled with "And Guest" people.
- The officiant and spouse are most often invited to your reception.
- You might allow your guests to bring their children to the wedding reception.
- The members of the band or the DJ are often

included in the caterer's headcount, as they
have to be fed too.
- The same goes with your photographer, videographer, and wedding coordinator.

Get It Right!

After you have built your guest list, be sure you have
the most current details on your guests:

- Their correct address and email (and phone, if
  appropriate).
- Their marital status (it would be a major *faux pas*
  to invite a couple you didn't know have gotten
  divorced, especially recently).
- The name of their current girlfriend, boyfriend,
  fiancé, or fiancée. (Hey, people do break
  up...you could unintentionally hurt someone if
  you didn't know they had called off their engagement or broken up recently!)
- The number and names of their kids. (Again, it
  would be a major *faux pas* if you invited parents
  and their two kids, leaving out their third child
  you didn't know existed.)
- The spellings of their names, and their titles, like
  Doctor.

Check with your parents and others to make sure
you have the essentials covered. Make no assump-
tions. Welcome to the world of attention to detail...

5

Formality and Style

Besides the size of your wedding, another key building block is the formality level. What's the level of formality that you both want for your day? Ultra-formal or more casual? These "categories" determine everything from the design of your wedding gown to what the groom wears to the location to the menu and décor...which always leads to your budget. In most cases, an ultra-formal wedding at an elegant ballroom will be vastly more expensive than a casual celebration in your home or on the beach. Your choices determine the path you'll take.

Here is where the two of you think about the formality levels and styles of weddings you've attended in the past. Which ones did you enjoy most? Which felt like the perfect match to your wedding dream? Were you uncomfortable dressed in a formal gown or tuxedo at a white-tie wedding? Did it all seem too exorbitant and not at all *you*?

Here are the formality categories in the wedding world. Check off the one that most appeals to your comfort level, personalities, and wishes for your big day:

Ultra-formal: White-tie or black-tie, with the men in tuxedos, all the women in long gowns, women (and perhaps men) wear gloves; over one-hundred-fifty guests; usually held in a house of worship or hotel ballroom; engraved invitations; an orchestra or band; fine crystal and china, the finest menu for a cocktail party, sit-down dinner and dessert—this is top of the line, almost reminiscent of a royal wedding.

Formal: The men in tuxedos, the women in long gowns; ceremony may be held in a house of worship or hotel ballroom; a band or orchestra entertains; an extravagant menu for the cocktail party, sit-down dinner and dessert; only slightly less formal than the ultra-formal wedding.

Semi-formal: Like the above two, only the women may wear cocktail-length dresses and the men may wear either tuxedos or matching dark suits. Cocktail parties and brunches are often in semi-formal mode, including outdoor weddings; usually a guest list of less than one hundred guests; smaller wedding parties; less elaborate décor.

Informal: Picture a casual beach wedding or backyard celebration, a more laid-back style with the men in khaki pants and button-down shirts and the women in sundresses; less elaborate décor; lighter fare, not necessarily a sit-down meal.

Of course, we'll get way more in-depth on wardrobe matching formality and style tips later, but I wanted to give you a visual so that you can select your desired formality level. It's very important at this stage of the game to be able to accurately state the formality when you're searching for locations and wedding experts.

6

Your Wedding Style

Do you have a picture in your head of your desired wedding's style? What does it look like? What do you see? Here are the top categories of wedding styles for you to consider and, ultimately, check off as your decision (again, key to your planning process and the creation of your wedding dream):

Traditional, Religious: The ceremony in a house of worship; the reception in a ballroom; a cocktail party, sit-down dinner and dessert hour; a DJ or band plus dancing and entertainment.

Traditional, Non-Religious: The same as above, with the ceremony outside of a house of worship.

Outdoor: The celebration is outdoors, most likely under a massive tent; formality ranges from ultra-formal to informal (it's your choice of design); the ceremony too may be held outdoors.

Beach: All or part of the wedding is held on the beach—one option is to have the ceremony on the beach and then the reception held inside a restaurant or ballroom.

Cocktail Party: No sit-down five-course dinner;

the entirety of the event is a cocktail party with passed hors d'oeuvres or a buffet, food stations, and a dessert buffet.

Brunch: The timing is earlier, and the buffet-style brunch may be held in a hotel ballroom or restaurant's private room; an extensive buffet is provided including food stations; entertainment may be a pianist or flutist.

Afternoon Tea: An elegant afternoon affair in which finger sandwiches, quiches, tea, and wines are on the menu; could be held at an estate home or bed and breakfast that matches the style of the upscale tea event.

Dessert and Champagne: Either formal or more laid-back, the celebration in the evening hours consists of a wide range of desserts and wedding cake, champagne or wines, coffee and after-dinner drinks.

Yacht: Your celebration will be held aboard a private or chartered yacht, a floating party on calm seas.

At Home: Either formal or informal, the wedding takes place at your home or the home of a family member or friend. (More on locations in chapter nine.)

Casual: Forget dressing up. This style brings everyone together in a much more laid-back way, perhaps for an outdoor cookout, a family-style dinner, or a buffet style gathering in a hall.

Destination: Whether in an island paradise or an exotic overseas city surrounded by history and architecture and a different culture—or just a few hours away at a beach or mountain resort, this style takes you and your handful of guests away from it all. Also called a getaway wedding.

Ethnic: The ceremony and/or reception contains plenty of cultural elements: décor, music, language, rituals, or menu items. The entire wedding could be in your ethnic theme, such as Asian or Polish, or just elements of it. Or, it could be an ethnic theme that's not even of your own heritage—you just love the style, such as a Moroccan theme, for instance.

Theme: You've built your wedding around a theme, choosing your décor, colors, menu, entertainment, favors, drinks, cake, flowers, invitations, and anything else to match your chosen theme for the day, reflecting who you are as a couple, perhaps the places you love, etc. Here are some ideas for possible themes:

An Evening in Tuscany
Shakespearean "Midsummer Night's Dream"
Arabian Nights
Under the Sea
Shooting Stars
1920s Speakeasy
USO Tour
The Golden Age of Hollywood
Disney Cinderella Theme
Winter Wonderland
Autumn in New England
Halloween
Mardi Gras
Fiesta
Renaissance
Tropical Beach Party (indoors or outside—fun for a cold January wedding date!)

## 7

Creating Your Budget

Weddings are expensive, but at any budget level, you *can* create the wedding of your dreams.

To get you started, mark the financial sharing plan that best fits your current situation:

__We'll pay for the wedding on our own, with no financial help from others.

__We'll stick with the traditional list of who pays for what? (See pages 54–57 for the age-old list of "how it's done.")

✓ We'll partner up with both sets of parents, as full planning and paying partners (which, by the way, is the case in most wedding planning teams these days).

__We have a generous benefactor, like a grandparent, offering to pay for the whole thing.

__We won a reality show, and the network is paying for the wedding.

Just kidding on that last one! No matter who is writing the checks, you'll still need to create and stick to a budget for your wedding. Your whole team needs to stick to the budget and communicate well about money, or else you have problems ahead. Money is the number one fight factor in wedding teams, so clear the air now with set guidelines on who's paying for what, and what will be spent.

Your Priority List

The first step in creating your budget is deciding which portions of your wedding are the most important to you, it just takes smooth handling of your budget priorities to make your dreams come true.

Here, you'll check off the budget categories that will become the top priorities for your wedding budget:

__Your gown
✓The flowers
__The cake
✓Reception catering
__Entertainment
__Invitations
✓Photography
__Videography
__Your rings
__Limousines
__tuxedos
__Favors and gifts
__Other:
__Other:
__Other:

Now that you have your most top priorities in mind, you can talk with the other members on your team about who will help you achieve which portions of the wedding, letting them know your top visions for the day.

WHO PAYS FOR WHAT?

Here is the traditional list that wedding teams have looked to for decades upon decades when trying to find the rules of who pays. Of course, like today's couples, you can decide to personalize this list and let anyone pay for the portion they can or want to cover. I've included it here to get you thinking...in a few pages, you'll be able to customize your wedding budget.

The Bride Pays For:
- The groom's wedding ring
- The groom's wedding gift
- The bridesmaids' gifts and Maid of Honor gift
- Medical examination and blood test for the marriage license, as required by the state
- Stationery for after the wedding

The Groom Pays For:
- The bride's engagement ring
- The bride's wedding ring
- The bride's wedding gift
- His own tuxedo, shoes, accessories or other wedding day wardrobe
- Gifts for his ushers, groomsmen, and Best Man

- The bride's bouquet
- The bride's going-away corsage or bouquet
- Corsages for the mothers, stepmothers, grand-mothers, and other honored women
- Boutonnieres for male wedding party members and fathers
- Medical examination and blood test for the marriage license
- The marriage license
- The officiant's fee
- The honeymoon

The Bride's Family Pays For:
- The engagement party
- The wedding coordinator (if applicable)
- Ceremony cost: location, music, rentals, and all related expenses
- Entire cost of reception, including catering, wedding cake, desserts, beverages, entertainment, decor, etc.
- Bride's gown, veil, shoes, and all accessories
- A wedding gift for the bride and groom
- Wedding invitations, Save the Date cards, and announcements
- Postage for the invitations, announcements, and other mailed items
- The bridesmaids' bouquets
- The flower girls' bouquets
- Transportation for the wedding day
- Bridal brunch on the morning of the wedding

- Photography
- Videography
- Floral décor
- Favors
- Special, sentimental items: unity candle, toasting flutes, ring pillow, money purse, etc.
- Their own wedding day wardrobes: dress, tuxedo rental, accessories, shoes, etc.
- Taxes and tips
- Travel and lodging for their guests (optional)

The Groom's Family Pays For:
- Rehearsal expenses
- The rehearsal dinner, including menu, drinks, invitations, décor, etc.
- Wedding gift for the bride and groom
- Their own wedding wardrobes: gown, tuxedo rental, shoes, accessories, etc.
- Travel and lodging for groom's family members (optional)
- Special sentimental items: unity candle, toasting flutes, ring pillow, etc.
- Taxes and tips

The Attendants Pay For:
- Wedding wardrobe and accessories
- Fittings and alterations
- Wedding day salon trip for hair, nails, etc.
- Their own travel and lodging expenses (if not complimentary)

- Wedding gift for bride and groom
- Showers
- Bachelor or bachelorette parties

The Bride and Groom Pay For:
- Gifts for wedding party and parents
- Gifts for all that helped with the wedding
- Extra expenses not covered by the parents' budget

If this arrangement sounds good to you, then you're all set to start talking details. Use the budget checklist on the following pages to keep track of everything.

Before You Start...

Remember that your initial budget figures could change throughout the course of planning. Your priorities might shift, and you might find items and services for far less than you had estimated. So use pencil to work this checklist and go with the flow as the numbers come pouring in. Things will change, but you'll be on top of it all.

Tipping Chart

While you're free to tip according to level of service, such as more if your waiters went above and beyond the call of duty, here are the usual figures for tipping at weddings:

__Officiants: $25 to $50 tip (in some regions, this can be $100 or more!)

__Ceremony site staff: $20 to $30 per person

___Organists and ceremony musicians: $20 to $50, depending on length of service

___Site manager: 15 to 20 percent of entire bill for the reception

___Waiters: $20 to $40 each, depending upon quality of service *or* 15 percent of catering bill

___Bartenders: 15 to 20 percent of liquor bill, more if they really pleased your guests

___Coat check: $1 to $2 per coat

___Valets: $1 to $2 per car

___Restroom attendants: $1 to $2 per guest in attendance

___Limousine drivers: 15 to 20 percent of transportation bill (Check to see if tip is already included in the contract first! If so, then on-the-day tip may be smaller as a token.)

___Delivery workers: $15 each if just dropping items off, $25 each if dropping off and setting up to great extent; more so if they're transporting a LOT of items.

___Tent assemblers, rental agency assemblers, and lighting assemblers: $20 each

___Cleanup crew: $20 each

___Entertainers: $25 to $30 each

___Beauty experts: 15 to 20 percent of beauty salon bill

___Baby-sitters: $30 to $40 each, plus a gift, in addition to their hourly wages; more if baby-sitter is putting in extra hours or caring for several children

__Event planner: 10 to 20 percent of your bill, *depending on the terms of contract.*

__Housekeeping attendants for guests' hotel rooms (Leave a note for guests *not* to tip the housekeeping staff—you'll take care of it!), $5 to $10 per day, per room

Who Is Not Tipped?

- Florist
- Cake baker
- Photographer
- Videographer
- Civil officiants

Fill individual envelopes with the appropriate amount of tip, label the envelopes according to recipient category or name, and then hand these off to the Best Man or a parent who will take care of tipping on the wedding day.

Part Two

When and Where?

8

Your Wedding Date

Choosing the perfect wedding date entails more than just finding both a ceremony site and a reception site with coordinating available dates. It has everything to do with which *season* you have in mind. Do you want to be a June bride with an outdoor summer wedding? Or do you prefer an autumn day with milder weather and a palette of colors on the trees? Here is where you'll start off with the season and then progress to find the calendar date for your big day.

The Four Seasons
A Spring or Summer Wedding

- Warm weather
- Possibilities for an outdoor or beach wedding
- Peak wedding season
- Seasonal flowers
- Guests with kids can more easily attend due to vacation time

An Autumn Wedding

- Colorful fall foliage on the trees
- Possible summery weather from an "Indian summer"
- Not competing with a crowded summer wedding season nor the winter holidays
- Just on outer edge of peak wedding season
- Milder weather
- Seasonal fall menu items and flowers

A Winter Wedding

- Lower off-season wedding prices
- No competition with summer weddings
- Make holiday time extra-festive
- Guests with kids might have available vacation time to attend
- Family might already be traveling to the area for the holidays with relatives
- Winter wonderland décor ideas
- Makes use of New Year's Eve or Valentine's Day

Dawn and Gary's Story

"We chose February for our wedding, thinking that we'd get lower prices for our wedding. But we got so much more. Our guests told us that our wedding brightened their moods during that very bleak winter season. It was something exciting to look forward to as we all awaited spring."

—*Dawn and Gary from New Jersey*

Peak wedding season is May through September, when the weather is most likely to be mild and comfortable. Since most couples want an ideal weather day, they look within the bounds of peak season. Wedding experts also know that to be the case, so they price their wedding services to suit demand, which often means you'll find higher prices within these months than in, say, January or April. Of course, the difference is not that grand, so don't count out the peak months. Just be aware as you search for the ideal wedding date for your wedding vision. You're about to get into finding those coordinating ceremony and reception site dates, so here's the next step...

DAY OF THE WEEK

Don't assume it's always going to be a Saturday. It very well could be, but you might also consider a Friday night wedding to make great use of special site discounts or your guests' schedules. Here are the dates and times you might consider:

- ✓ Saturday evening
- ✓ Saturday afternoon (Yes, you can do formal in the afternoon!)
- __ Friday night
- __ Sunday afternoon
- __ Thursday night (or another weekday night, provided your guests all live in the area and can make it on a non-peak night)
- __ Sunday night, when it's a three-day weekend such as Columbus Day or Memorial Day weekend

When you're trying to match a reception site with your dream ceremony site, it's nice to know you do have options!

Dates to Stay Away From

Obviously you might think twice about booking your wedding on Friday the thirteenth for superstitious reasons, but there are other "yikes" days you might want to steer clear of. Some dates on the calendar may be difficult to consider, whether it's a difficult anniversary date like September 11 or the anniversary of a parent's or sibling's death, or the day that *would* have been your sister's wedding anniversary had she not gotten divorced last year (Yikes!). Couples have dates they wouldn't consider, like when they're studying for the bar exam, so use this checklist to record the dates you wouldn't consider:

__Superbowl Sunday: It's consistently the *least* popular day for weddings!

__

__

What Time Is It?

The time of day correlates to the wedding's formality and style. Those are the rules, and they're not going away any time soon. So check off the following time and descriptions that are on your wish list:

Type of Reception	Time of Day (Start Time)
Brunch	11 a.m.–1 p.m.
Luncheon	12 noon–2 p.m.
Tea	3 p.m.–4 p.m.
Cocktail Party	4 p.m.–7 p.m.
Dinner	5 p.m.–8 p.m.
Champagne and Dessert	8 p.m.–10 p.m.
Late Night	9 p.m.–12 midnight or later
Overnight	late-night start, running into the next day

DATE, TIME, AND SITE COORDINATION WORKSHEET

You'll have to find coordinating days and times at your potential ceremony and reception sites in order to set your wedding date. It all works together.

In the next chapter, you'll find out more about scouting out the ideal places to get married and to celebrate, so consider these to be tag team chapters. You'll use them together to line up the perfect place at the perfect time. Once you have contender locations, use this checklist to find the perfect dual-fit for the dates and backup dates you have in mind:

Wedding Date and Time Possibility #1:

Wedding Date and Time Possibility #2:

Wedding Date and Time Possibility #3:

Wedding Date and Time Possibility #4:

Wedding Date and Time Possibility #5:

Wedding Date and Time Possibility #6:

Ceremony Site #1 (C1):

Ceremony Site #2 (C2):

Ceremony Site #3 (C3):

Ceremony Site #4 (C4):

Ceremony Site #5 (C5):

Ceremony Site #6 (C6):

Reception Site #1 (R1):

Reception Site #2 (R2):

Reception Site #3 (R3):

Reception Site #4 (R4):

Reception Site #5 (R5):

Reception Site #6 (R6):

Example

	R1	R2
C1	*Both OK on June 26, 4 p.m.*	*Both OK on June 19, 4 p.m.*
C2	*Both OK on June 26, 4 p.m.*	*Both OK on August 7, noon*

	R1	R1	R1	R1	R1	R1
C1						
C2						
C1						
C2						
C1						
C2						

Remember, you can have a half hour to an hour (or two) of time between the end of the ceremony and the start of the reception, which gives you breathing room to take your post-wedding pictures, have a toast or two with your bridal party and parents, etc. So don't worry if the times don't match up precisely. Your guests can entertain themselves at a nearby lounge until the cocktail hour starts.

Your Wedding Date and Time:

9

Your Location

The perfect wedding requires the perfect setting for both your ceremony and reception as well as for all other events, like your rehearsal dinner, bridal breakfasts, and even the idyllic place where you'll take your post-ceremony pictures.

YOUR CEREMONY LOCATION

When you are scouting for a religious ceremony location, here are the steps you'll take:

- ✓ Line up the possibilities, getting recommendations from friends or family on beautiful and welcoming houses of worship for you to consider.
- ✓ Call the church or synagogue office to make an appointment with an officiant.
- ✓ Inquire about application requirements, such as your divorce papers or annulment certificate from a previous marriage, death certificate from a previous spouse, even your baptism certificate, if needed.
- ___ Inquire about any essays or paperwork you'll have to fill out—many houses of worship want to

know who you are and what you believe, so they'll ask you about yourselves.

___Inquire about premarital counseling or classes, and scheduling of when you could attend.

___Tour the ceremony site to check out the following:

- *Space*
- *Plenty of natural light*
- *Candlelight ambiance*
- *Architecture*
- *Acoustics*
- *Décor, such as color of carpet, icons*
- *Balcony*
- *Organ music available*
- *Choir available*
- *Restrooms available*
- *Parking available*
- *Separate dressing room for bride*

___Interview the officiant to be sure he or she is okay by *you*, if you like his or her style. This is the person who will be running the show, the person attached to that great church you adore; so make sure you like your officiant.

___Inquire about the site's restrictions, such as no pictures allowed, no flash photography allowed, no secular music allowed, décor must be approved, your vows must be approved, no changing the wedding ceremony script, etc.

NON-RELIGIOUS SITES

Some couples choose, either of their own volition or due to a shortage of available religious locations, to marry outside of a house of worship. Some ideas for these locations are (check those that interest you):

__A separate hotel ballroom from your reception
ballroom

__The hotel's atrium or gardens

__Outdoor grounds, such as at a park, country
club, botanical gardens, historic estate, etc.

__Your front yard (with the reception in your
backyard)

__On the beach

__At a gazebo in a park

__A trellis area at a botanical park or arboretum

__The grounds of a bed and breakfast

__Restaurant party room with a glass wall overlooking
the ocean or mountains

__Mountaintop at sunset

__Civil ceremony setting, such as in a judge's cham-
bers or in a decorated common room at town hall

2-for-1 Setting

Of course, your ceremony and reception could take
place in the same location, so look for a separate
area in any gorgeous reception setting where the
managers could arrange chairs and an aisle for your
own personalized ceremony space right on the same
grounds. The plus side? One location to decorate,
time saved by not having to travel from one location
to the other, less driving for your guests, and no
waiting for the reception to begin!

Places to Take Pictures

Of course, the site of your wedding will provide a gorgeous backdrop to every element of your day—whether it's the grounds of an estate home, the view of the sunset from the restaurant terrace, a marble staircase that you will descend as husband and wife. But there is yet another location to select: the place where your post-ceremony pictures will be taken.

In my town, we have a garden gazebo in the park. Each weekend, brides and grooms and their wedding parties literally line up to have their wedding photos taken at The Gazebo. It's a tradition here.

Here are your checklist steps for finding and securing the perfect picture-taking location for your wedding day:

___Find potential locations by asking your recently married friends where they posed.

___Ask your wedding coordinator, photographer, videographer, and florist for suggestions—they may have worked in some gorgeous places in the past.

___Check online for your regional magazine's website, in which you might find articles on the top ten scenic views in the state.

___Check your state park website for pictures and information on specific areas, ponds, parks, and places specified as scenic views, plus links to their information offices.

___Spend a few Sundays driving through the area, looking for scenic views, park areas, horse farms, bed and breakfasts, and other ideal spots. Very often, you'll find the perfect place by surprise.

___Make sure the site is nearby; you don't want to take an hour's drive out of the way right after your ceremony just to stand by a nice field of flowers.

___Check the site for safety factors now and right before the wedding.

___Contact the park rangers or the site's information offices to inquire about permits and site fees. Some botanical gardens and other sites will let you come on their grounds (even after hours!) for a specified time of picture taking.

___Fill out an application, book the space, and get a contract in hand.

___Call the town hall to ask if permits are needed for your town park setting.

___Get printed directions from the site, or create printed directions for your photographer, limousine drivers, etc. from an online map-making site (like MapQuest).

___Choose a Plan B in case of rain, a different place indoors that is just as lovely, a place you'll be pleased to have as your backup pictures location.

Final site chosen:

Part Three

Planning Your Ceremony

Ceremony Basics

You've already found the location for your ceremony, and filled out all the paperwork for your "eligibility" to be married there. In case your site isn't a house of worship that comes with its own officiant, we'll first cover the steps you'll take to find and hire a licensed officiant to conduct your ceremony.

WHO'S MARRYING YOU

If indeed you won't go the religious route, then you'll search through your state-approved list of officiants to find the professional who is licensed to seal your deal. I say state-approved because marriage laws are different in many states, even from one county to the next. To avoid any confusion, go right to your town hall or county courthouse and ask for the most current list of approved wedding officiant candidates. You may find the following:

- The mayor
- Superior court judges
- Appellate court judges

- A member of the town council
- And others

Some states do *not* have a Justice of the Peace, so your search might have to go through the courthouse.

Or, you could do some research on an independent minister, one who is licensed to conduct marriage ceremonies, of course. Here is where you figure out what you're looking for in your officiant. Check off the qualities you have in mind:

✓ Religious

___ Secular

___ Interfaith

___ Nondenominational

___ Orthodox

___ New Age/Spiritual

___ Performs ceremonies outdoors or outside a house of worship

___ Is willing to tailor our ceremony to our wording wishes

✓ Provides sample ceremony wording scripts

✓ Has a valid license to conduct ceremonies

✓ Is affordable

✓ Is available on our wedding date

___ Can travel to our wedding site

___ Other: (fill in any specifics you have in mind for your ideal wedding officiant)

The Qualities of a Great Officiant

- Answers all of your questions thoroughly
- Easygoing and approachable
- Lighthearted
- Explains the church's rules in completion
- Listens to your ceremony requests
- Never makes you feel judged for not being a member of the church
- Doesn't push membership or beliefs on you
- Speaks encouragingly to you both
- Has a great presence, makes you feel comfortable
- Helps you personalize your ceremony to include your values and beliefs
- Provides sample ceremony "scripts" and vows, along with musical lists
- Accommodates your schedule for meetings, such as agreeing to meet with you after work hours
- Allows you to see him or her at work, performing another wedding
- Tells you what he or she will wear to your wedding
- Tells you "the door is always open…"

YOUR CEREMONY'S STYLE

Check off the qualities that you want your ceremony to have: (Important, so that your chosen officiant can guide you in the right direction)

___Very religious, high mass, over an hour

___Religious, but without the high mass

___Formal, by the book

___Formal, personalized

___Very musical—we want lots of music breaks

___Ethnic rituals included

___Religious rituals included

___Interfaith led by two officiants, each dividing up the ceremony

___Very spiritual, including handfasting and spiritual rituals

___Light and humorous

___Bilingual

___Quick and informal

___Sentimental tributes included, such as to a departed parent

___Unconventional

___Reverent

___Just like our parents' weddings

___Other: (fill in your own chosen descriptions and share this with your officiant for ceremony building)

Creating Your Ceremony

You're building the heart of your wedding day right here with the words, music, and rituals you choose to convey your deepest beliefs about marriage and your love for one another.

THE MUSIC

It's often the first thing your guests notice even before they enter your ceremony site: the lovely music playing from inside. It sets the tone and the mood and speaks of who *you* are by selecting the songs played on your day. This is the soundtrack of your wedding day from moment one.

Take a Listen

Visit www.weddingchannel.com to actually *listen* to many songs through their link with amazon.com, and find many additional classical and contemporary songs for your consideration.

Check off the songs you'd like to request of your musicians that day:

Prelude (music playing before the ceremony begins, as guests arrive and take their seats):

___"Air" from *Water Music*, by George Handel

___"Allegro" from *Brandenberg concerto #4 in G*, by Johann Sebastian Bach

___*Clair de Lune* by Claude Debussy

___*Moonlight Sonata* by Ludwig van Beethoven

___*Swan Lake* by Tchaikovsky

___*The Four Seasons* by Vivaldi

___"Waltz" from *Sleeping Beauty*, by Tchaikovsky

___"Waltz in A Flat" by Johannes Brahms

___"Water Music Suite No. 1 in F: Menuet" by George Handel

___"Wedding Cantata" by Johann Sebastian Bach

___Additional songs you'd like for your prelude:

Processional (music playing as your wedding party—and you—make your entrance down the aisle):

___"Arioso" by Johann Sebastian Bach

___"Blue Danube Waltz" by Strauss

___"Canon in D" by Johann Pachelbel

___"Jesu, Joy of Man's Desiring" by Johann Sebastian Bach

___"Romance" from *Eine Kleine Nachtmusik*, by Wolfgang Amadeus Mozart

___"Trumpet Voluntary" from the *Prince of Denmark's March*, by Jeremiah Clarke

__"The Four Seasons" by Antonio Vivaldi

__"Water Music suite No. 2" by George Handel

__"Wedding March" from Lohengrin, by Wagner

__Additional songs you'd like for your processional:

Interlude (music playing during any rituals or during music-appropriate portions of the ceremony):

__"Alleluia" by Johann Sebastian Bach

__"Ave Maria" by Franz Schubert

__"The Lord's Prayer" by Albert Hay Malone

__"Ode to Joy" by Ludwig van Beethoven

__"Spring" from *The Four Seasons*, by Antonio Vivaldi

__Additional songs you'd like for your interlude:

Recessional (music playing as the ceremony concludes and you lead your wedding party and guests back up the aisle):

__"Hallelujah Chorus" from *The Messiah*, by George Handel

__"Hornpipe" from *Water Music*, by George Handel

__"Ode to Joy" by Ludwig van Beethoven

__"Spring" from *The Four Seasons*, by Antonio Vivaldi

__"Wedding March" from *A Midsummer Night's Dream*, by Felix Mendelssohn

__"Wedding March" from the *Marriage of Figaro*, by Wolfgang Amadeus Mozart

__Additional songs you'd like for your recessional:

You might choose to forego the classics and select more contemporary music, songs your guests will recognize and perhaps even songs that have a special place in your history as a couple (as in, the first song you ever slow-danced to together). Check the following tunes you favor, or check out your own CD collection for unique ideas that you can weave into your ceremony pattern:

__"All I Ask of You" from *Phantom of the Opera,* by Sir Andrew Lloyd Webber

__"At Last" by Etta James

__"Cross My Heart" by George Strait

__"My Romance" by Rosemary Clooney

__"The Best is Yet to Come" by Frank Sinatra (a favorite for the Recessional)

__"The First Time Ever I Saw Your Face" by Roberta Flack

__"The Prayer" by Celine Dion and Andrea Boccelli

__"True Colors" by Phil Collins or Cyndi Lauper

__"True Love" by Rebecca St. James

__"What a Wonderful World" by Louis Armstrong (a favorite pick for the Prelude)

__"You Are So Beautiful" by Joe Cocker

__Instrumentals by George Winston

__Your choices of contemporary music for your ceremony:

Special Songs:

Here is where you'll record the titles of special songs you'd like played during spotlight moments in the ceremony:

When the mothers are seated:

When the groom enters the room:

When you make your entrance:

During the lighting of the unity candle:

During the exchange of peace and greetings:

During any special tribute to departed family members:

Other:

READINGS

If your ceremony will include inspirational readings or passages of scripture, poetry, quotes, or notable words of wisdom from your favorite author (or aunt), take some time to research the wealth of wonderful words you may use to speak your hearts.

Religious and Spiritual:

- The Bible (Psalms, Ecclesiastes, Song of Songs, the Book of Ruth, the Book of John, Ephesians, and especially Corinthians)
- Sheva B'rachot (The Jewish Seven Blessings)
- The Tao Te Ching
- The Book of Common Prayer
- The Prophet by Khalil Gibran
- The works of Lao Tzu
- The works of Rumi
- The works of Marianne Williamson

Poets and Authors:

- William Shakespeare
- Robert Browning
- Elizabeth Barrett Browning
- Sir Philip Sidney
- Christina Rossetti
- Charlotte Brontë
- Emily Brontë
- Walt Whitman
- Ralph Waldo Emerson
- Rainer Maria Wilke
- Pablo Neruda
- Willa Cather
- e.e. cummings
- Emily Dickinson
- John Keats
- John Milton
- Others:

More Contemporary Authors and Poets:

- Marianne Williamson
- Maya Angelou
- Nikki Giovanni
- Anne Morrow Lindbergh
- Leo Buscaglia
- Martha Beck
- Don Miguel Ruiz
- Others:

Word Hunt

These authors' and writers' names plugged into any good search engine will turn up gorgeous, timeless romantic writings, inspirational quotes, and sayings that will add depth and meaning to your ceremony.

One great source for finding quotes and lines from classic poetry is www.BrainyQuotes.com. That will get you started in fine style.

WORDS FROM YOUR LOVED ONES

You can quote your own loved ones in your ceremony. Here is where you'll record any quotes or sayings from your own circle that you'd like to use:

-
-
-
-
-
-
-

WORDS TO YOUR LOVED ONE:
YOUR WEDDING VOWS

Here, you'll check off the steps that you'll take in the process of writing perhaps *the* most important words of your entire day:

___Research vow ideas in books and at bridal websites.

___Sit down together to discuss what you both want to express and promise to one another.

___Decide on a level of formality (i.e., will you be

very serious, or will you use your own sense of humor in a respectable way).

__Write your first draft.

__Decide if you want to write your vows together, or write them separately and surprise one another on the big day.

__Decide if you want to write one set of vows that you'll both repeat to one another, or if you'd both like to create your own individual expressions.

__Edit down your vows to capture the essence of what you want to say.

__Submit your vows to your officiant for approval, if that's what's required at your house of worship.

__Practice reading your vows aloud, timing the length of them. Keep it short, sweet, and to the point.

__Practice reading your vows aloud, to make sure that you're comfortable with what you're saying.

__Print your final vows up on a card to be handed to the officiant for your repeating upon his or her prompts, or handed to you for your own reading.

__Decide if you want to memorize your vows (but keep that card handy in case you need it during a case of the nerves).

__Create a keepsake-printed copy of your vows on parchment paper for display in your home or in your wedding picture albums.

Taking Vows with Others

It might not just be the two of you promising to love, adore, support, and cherish one another until the end of time. You might also choose to include the following additional vow ceremonies:

_Vows you take with your children, etc.

_Vows your guests will repeat to their own partners.

_Vows your guests may take, at the prompting of the officiant, to always support the two of you in your partnership.

RITUALS

From the ring exchange to the lighting of the unity candle, wedding ceremonies are rich with ritual, tradition, and symbolism—whether religious, spiritual, or cultural. Check off any marriage rite rituals that you'd like to include in your ceremony, and add additional ideas of your own:

✓Single ring ceremony

_Double ring ceremony

✓Lighting of the unity candle

_Circling the altar a set number of times

_Wearing crowns

_Wearing wreaths of olive leaves

_Handfasting

_Entwining your hands with a rosary or cord

_Food ceremonies

_Wine ceremonies

_Tea ceremonies

_Lighting incense

_Breaking the glass

___Ringing bells

___The playing of drums in a steady heartbeat rhythm

✓The presentation of flowers to the mothers

___The presentation of flowers (or a gift offering)
to an icon of a saint

___The exchange of greetings

___Allowing guests to speak or participate in rituals

___Jumping the broom

___Others:

Your Ceremony Outline

___Make a list of all the elements of your ceremony
in order, including any details that go with
them, such as the names of readers, musicians,
or the officials.

___Make a list of everyone you'll have in your receiv-
ing line, including the order in which you will
stand.

___Determine how you'll exit with a flourish, which
could include:

Item:

___Birdseed

___Rose petals

___Confetti

___Bubbles

___Sparklers

___Bells

___Other:

(Package the toss-it items in advance).

Item:

___Tulle pouches (A square of sheer fabric cut into squares, with a dollop of birdseed in the center, edges drawn up, and tied into a pouch with lengths of color-coordinated ribbon.)

___Victorian cones (Take a piece of colored or graphic paper and roll it up into the shape of an ice cream cone, with one end open. Staple the edges and fill the container with rose petals.)

___Individual sticks of sparklers might be tied together with a color-coordinated ribbon.

___Small bottles of bubble mixture can be decorated with a computer printout label of your names, picture, or a bridal icon like wedding bells. The top might be tied with a ribbon bow.

___Small cardboard gift boxes containing birdseed might be decorated with a label or with a stick-on colored bow on top.

Packaging Source

Check out www.bayleysboxes.com for creative and inexpensive container ideas, like clear packages, boxes folded to form pyramids, or rose-topped circles, etc.)

Part Four

Your Wedding Gown; His Dashing Tuxedo

12

Selecting Your Wedding Gown

Your first order of business is matching the style of your gown to the formality of your wedding. Use the basic formality chart below to make sure you're considering dresses that fit your day perfectly, and get additional, personalized advice from your gown stylist:

Ultra-formal (white-tie and black-tie weddings):
- Full-length ballgown (no cocktail-length)
- Elbow-length gloves mandatory for ultra-formal weddings
- Train
- Headpiece and veil

Formal, evening, and daytime:
- Full-length gown or ballgown
- Veil and headpiece
- Train decision is up to you

Semi-formal:
- Full-length gown, ballgown, or...
- Cocktail-length gown

- Veil and headpiece, or just a headpiece
- Train is usually short, if you have one at all

Informal:

- Cocktail-length dress, or...
- Knee-length dress
- Dressy pantsuit
- Usually flowers in hair, headpiece, or jeweled hair clips

Casual:

- Knee-length dress
- Sundress
- Bathing suit and sarong
- Flowers in hair or jeweled hair clips

Your chosen gown formality level:

Your search for the perfect gown starts with an initial reconnaissance through the following expected (and some surprising) sources:

✓ Bridal magazines
✓ Bridal websites
___ Individual gown designers' websites
___ Designer trunk sales
___ Department stores' formal gown departments (and their online sites)
✓ Bridal expos or showcases
___ Fashion week coverage on television

_____Books about choosing a wedding gown, put out
by the bridal magazines

_____Fashion magazines ("I want the off-white gown
Jennifer Garner is wearing in this picture from
the Oscars!")

___Other...

Your Gown's Color

There's no need anymore to limit yourself to "vir-
ginal white" only—today's wedding gowns, even for
first-time brides, come in a range of hues:

___White

___Eggshell

___Off-white

___Cream or ivory

___Blush pastel

___White with pastel beading or accents

___Off-white with pastel beading or accents

✓White with bright embroidery or accents

___Off-white with bright embroidery or accents

___Metallics, like a smooth light copper or light silver

___Bright or rich colors (Perhaps for a second
wedding)

___Other:

Silhouettes

Do you want the puffy princess gown with the wide,
sweeping skirt, or a slinky sheath?

___Traditional ballgown

✓Fitted bodice with A-line skirt

___Straight line silhouette

___Fitted sheath

___Other:

Gown Lengths

✓Floor-length—the skirt just touches the floor

___Ballet-length—the skirt reaches to your ankles

___Intermission-length—the end of the skirt is at calf-length

___Hi-low length—the back of the skirt reaches to the floor or ankles, while the front of the skirt is intermission-length

___Street-length—the skirt reaches to your knees

Show Some Shoulder?

This category decides your skin factor...

✓Strapless

___Low neckline, such as a princess or sweetheart neckline, scoop, or square-neck that shows off a degree of cleavage

___High neckline, demure and classic

___Halter-top

___Open back

___Bare arms or covered arms?

___Legs showing, such as with a shorter skirt or a dramatic slit up the leg

___Cut-outs covered with illusion netting, such as a section that shows off your midriff, or designs up your legs, or a netting-covered back

___Other:

The style and formality of your gown—not to mention your comfort level with dragging a few yards of material behind you as you walk and turn—will determine which length of train completes your gown's look:

__Sweep-length—the train reaches down just to the length of the floor

__Watteau-length—the train is attached at your shoulders and reaches to the floor

✓Court-length—the train reaches out one foot behind you

__Chapel-length—the train reaches out three to four feet behind you (this is the most popular length)

__Semi-cathedral length—the train reaches out four to six feet behind you

__Cathedral length—the train reaches six to eight feet behind you, for the most formal of weddings

__Royal Cathedral length (also known as Traditional Royal)—the train reaches ten feet or more

Heirloom Gowns

You do have the option to use a gown already owned by your mother or grandmother, even your future in-laws. Just have it professionally cleaned and fitted, and you've saved yourself thousands of dollars. Not to mention added a degree of sentimentality to your wedding day. Some brides hire a seamstress to *copy* an heirloom gown that's just not in that great of a condition, *or* they hire a seamstress to use individual elements from several heirloom gowns. A great seamstress can work miracles.

YOUR GOWN SHOPPING EXPEDITION

First, you have to find the ideal gown shop. Again, ask friends and family for referrals.

- ✓ Make sure the place has a terrific selection of the latest gowns, that the help is friendly and knowledgeable, and that their contract is professional.
- ✓ Check out several shops to find the best one.
- ___ Don't forget to bring along shoes in the heel height you'll wear on the wedding day. (For fittings, bring the correct heel height shoes and the bra and undergarments you'll wear on the wedding day—that's how your seamstress gets the perfect fit.)

Your chosen gown shop is:

Name of salesperson:

Your final gown choice is:

Your Gown Ordering Worksheet

Designer Name:

Dress Style # or Name:

Size:

Price:

Deposit Due:

Deposit Due Date:

Date Deposit Paid:

Final Payment Due:

Final Payment Due Date:

Delivery Date:

Final Payment Made:

Notes on Changes to Style:

Extras Included:

Alterations Included?

ALTERATIONS SCHEDULE

Whether they're free from the gown shop, or you'll hire your own professional seamstress to fit the gown just right, record your fitting schedule here:

Seamstress Name:

Address:

Phone:

Fax:

Price:

Deposit:

Date Final Payment Due:

Final Payment Made:

Date	Time	Who's Going With You
Final Fitting		

YOUR VEIL AND HEADPIECE

Decide which type of headpiece and veil you'd like...

Headpiece:

__Tiara

__Headband

__Clip

__Comb

__Plain and simple

__Adorned with gemstones or flowers

__Other:

Veil:

✓Elbow-length—a shorter veil that is popular for less formal wedding gowns

__Fingertip-length—for formal and semi-formal weddings, this veil reaches to the end of your fingertips

__Chapel-length—a longer veil, reaching to the floor and perhaps beyond

___Cathedral-length—the longest, this one reaches at least half a foot to a foot beyond the train

Tips on Veils

- Always choose a veil that compliments the design of your dress—get expert style help to accentuate your bodice.
- You don't have to match a long veil with a long train—it all depends on how each length of veil looks with the design of your gown.
- A long veil of sheer tulle will still show off the accents on the back of your dress.
- If you have a wide waist, don't choose a veil that ends at waist-length. That look will "cut you in half" visually.
- If you're petite, under 5'3", don't choose a veil that ends at calf-length. A longer veil will heighten you.
- Decide if you want a regular veil, a shimmer veil, or a veil with beading or crystals sewn on.

Other Accessories

Of course, you'll have your own accessories to get, in order to perfect your wedding day look. Record your choices here as you keep track of your essentials:

✓ Shoes:
✓ Jewelry:
✓ Undergarments:
___Crinoline:
___Hosiery:
___Gloves:
✓ Hair clips and décor:
___Other:

Your Emergency Bag

Toting a Kate Spade bridal purse could complete your stylish wedding day look, and you might have a satin gift bag ready to hold your cash envelope wedding gifts. But the most important bag of the day is your emergency bag, or even in a bridal-theme gift shopping bag that can be hidden underneath your parents' dinner table:

__Breath mints or strips

__Tissues

__Pressed powder compact

__Lipstick or lip gloss

__Touchup eyeliner or mascara

__Emery board (in case you break a nail)

__Safety pins or travel sewing kit

__Travel-sized bottle of baby powder

__Eye drops or contact lens solution and contact lens kit

__Eyeglasses (just in case)

__Feminine products

__Travel mirror

__Cell phone and charger

__Medications—pain killer, allergy, insulin, bee sting kit, etc.

__A copy of this book, for easy look-up of your experts' phone numbers

__Extra stockings (in case of a run)

__Extra earrings set (in case you lose one of yours)

__Tweezers (in case of splinters)

__Band-aids (in case of blisters)

___Set of comfy shoes or ballet slippers to change into later in the night

___Hair brush

___Hair spray

___Fuel-cell-powered curling iron (My favorite wedding day tool to "spruce up" spiral curls and tendrils during the night.)

___Mosquito repellent spray (For evening hours at outdoor weddings, your bottle can be passed around to guests as well.)

___Stain remover wipes

___Other:

## 13

The Groom's Tuxedo and the Men's Wedding Day Look

What the groom wears on the wedding day is a classic part of your wedding vision, so start your search through wedding magazines and online with an eye toward what would look great on him and on the men in the wedding party, the fathers, and the ring bearer.

Your first choice is color. Select from the following to pick the perfect shade to suit the style of your wedding and coordinate well with what you and the women are wearing:

✓Classic black

__Gray

__Navy blue

__White

__Ivory

__Other:

And then select if you want:

✓Solid

__Pinstripe (for afternoon elegance)

Accessorize Your Men

Make sure they have matching:

- ☑ White shirts
- _Bow ties
- ☑ Long ties
- _Cravats
- _Ascots
- ☑ Vests
- _Cummerbunds
- _Socks (Instruct on sock color to ensure uniformity)
- _Cufflinks
- _Button covers
- _Pocket squares
- _Gloves (If a formal or military wedding where men wear gloves)
- _Ethnic accessories
- _Other:

WHERE TO FIND THE IDEAL TUXEDO RENTAL SHOP

Of course, you'll find your prime rental shop through...

- __Referrals from recently married friends and family
- __Your wedding coordinator
- __Bridal shows and expos
- __Your own contacts, such as the tuxedo shop the groom has used before
- __Personal tour of a nearby rental shop, noting styles, cleanliness, prices, a great reputation in town, etc.

Get Their Sizes

If any of the groomsmen or fathers live far away, and thus cannot attend the group shopping trip with the men to place their orders, have them send in official size cards. Expert tailors will measure the men's dimensions, and the men will then send their size cards to you for you to place their order. Shoe sizes included.

Who's returning them:

Notes:

Additional Items to Get

If you need to buy anything else for your men's wedding day look, record it here...

-
-
-

## 14

Gowns for Your Bridesmaids and Moms

Color is the first concern your bridesmaids have, so put all of your minds at ease by choosing a terrific color your maids will most likely be able to wear again. Here are a few to start with, and you'll fill in your own:

___Red

___Cranberry

___Black

___Navy or lighter blue

___Hunter or sage green

Your color choice: *Apple*

Now, you get to make their day even better with this next decision:

___I'll let the maids help select the gown

_/_I'll let the Maid of Honor help select the gown

___I'll let the maids choose their own style of gown as long as it's in the same exact color, or color range

___I'll let the maids wear their own gowns or dresses in the same color (like black), provided they check

with me first to okay formality, length, and style
___It's all my decision

WHERE TO SEARCH FOR DRESSES OR GOWNS

Here's your source list, so that you can plan your shopping excursions:

___Bridal magazines
___Bridal websites
___Gown designers' websites
___Department stores (or their websites)
___Department stores' prom gown section
___Designer outlets
___Designer sample sales (good if you have only one to two bridesmaids to outfit)
___Other:

ACCESSORIES

Your bridesmaids and Maid of Honor need, of course, to get matching accessories to complete their unified look as your bridal party. Mom, too, will need to organize her accessory search. Here's where you'll organize the group effort:

✓Jewelry (Matching sets of necklaces and earrings could be a thank-you gift from you.)

✓Shoes (Specify open- or closed-toe, a specific color—like black—or have a matching style dyed to order in one lot.)

___Gloves
___Hosiery (Your maids' legs should match shades.)

__Undergarments (They'll get these on their own, but you could point them to a great source for strapless bras.)

__Other:

## 15

Dressing the Little Ones

Check your wishes here, so that you can partner with the kids' parents to find and buy outfits and accessories for the littlest members of the wedding party:

FLOWER GIRLS
The girls will be dressed in:
__Full-length dresses
__Tea-length dresses
__Party dresses, new
__Party dresses they already own
__Costume (i.e. angel or fairy with gossamer wings)
__Other

Color selected:
Color of sash to add to a white party dress:

Where to Shop:
__Bridal salon
__Department store
__Kids' clothing store

___Kids' clothing outlet
   (Check www.outletbound.com for locations)
___Catalog
___Website
___Other:

Accessories Needed:
___Shoes (Color:_____)
   • New party flats
   • Party flats she already owns
   • Dyed shoes
   • Ballet slippers
   • Other
___Hosiery (Color and style:_____)
___Gloves (Color and size:_____)
___Jewelry
___Jacket
___Other:

RINGBEARERS
They Will Wear:
___Tuxedo to match the men
___Black pants, white shirt, rented or purchased matching tie
___Khaki pants, white shirt, and tie (for a more casual wedding)
___Costume
___Other:

Accessories Needed:

__Shoes (Size and color:_____)

__Tie

__Vest

__Cummerbund

__Socks

__Cufflinks

__Other:

Where to Shop:

__Tuxedo rental shop

__Department store

__Kids' clothing store

__Kids' clothing outlet (Check www.outletbound.com for locations)

__Catalog

__Website

__Other:

BABYSITTER CHECKLIST

It might be that the flower girls and ringbearer are too young to stay up late into the reception, or that you want to give *all* of your guests with kids a night out without the little ones. In any case, if you wish to hire babysitters, here is where you'll organize the details:

__# of sitters needed:

__Hours:

__# of kids being watched:

__Menu for the kids' meal and snacks:

__Drinks for the kids:

___Dessert for the kids:

___Activities planned:

___Movies

___Games

___Hired entertainers (puppetry, magicians, costumed characters, etc.)

___Crafts

___Other:

___Favors:

___Fees:

___Overtime fees:

___Tip and gift:

___Sitter's cell phone number:

___Sitter given an emergency number to contact you or parents

___Notes:

Part Five

Wedding Details

16

Your Wedding Rings

Here's where you'll choose and shop for your wedding band—as will your groom—so that you'll love the most important piece of jewelry you'll ever own.

Getting Ideas

Research the new crop of stylish and creative wedding rings online at jewelry sites and bridal websites. Flip through bridal magazines and cruise through jewelry stores for plenty of inspiration as you dream up the design of your ideal wedding bands. Or, visit such great sites as www.bluenile.com and www.adiamondisforever.com to actually *design* your own ring element by element. Print out your masterpieces and bring them to your jeweler for a custom job.

DESIGN AND STYLE

This section is for both of you to make your own choices regarding the style and design of your wedding bands.

Choosing Your Metals:

__Platinum

✓ White gold
__Sterling silver
__14-karat gold
__Other:

Choosing Your Stones:
__Diamonds
__Sapphires
__Rubies
__Emeralds
__Your birthstone
__Other

Matching Set?
__We'll buy a matching set of wedding bands
✓ We'll each choose our own separate styles

HEIRLOOM RINGS

Using heirloom rings—or parts of them—is a popular, budget-saving trend that also adds to your wedding bands the sentimental histories of your relatives.
Here are some ideas:

__Use an heirloom ring after getting it cleaned up
and polished.

__Take the gorgeous stones from an heirloom ring
and have them fitted into a new, more modern
ring setting.

__Use the stones from an heirloom piece of jewelry
(such as a pendant or a bracelet) and have them
reset into a new band.

___Get new stones for a stunning platinum heirloom setting.

___Take heirloom men's bands to the jeweler for a polish and refurbishing.

FINDING A FABULOUS JEWELER

The key to a wise wedding ring investment is finding the best jeweler out there—a company with great rings and great, reliable service. Here's how to find the ideal expert for this most important shopping task:

- Visit the jeweler your family uses. Your parents might have a long history with the reputable jeweler in town, and you might even snag a discount for being part of their network.

- Ask your recently married friends and family, or people you know who buy a *lot* of fine jewelry, for their recommendations. This is often the wisest way to go.

- Check with jewelry associations online, like the American Gem Society (www.ags.org) to find nearby recommended jewelers.

- Check out jewelry stores and review their selections, making sure you stick with shops that have been around a long time—not the one that just popped up at the mall and could be gone just as quickly.

Engraving

You might choose to have a special message engraved inside your wedding bands. Decide if you want your

initials, your wedding date, your nicknames, or some
romantic saying like "Always" or "Forever."

Your engraving wording:
The groom's engraving wording:

Appraisals and Insurance

__Be sure to get your rings independently
appraised at a site other than where you bought
it, and get the appraisal value in writing.

__Be sure to get your rings covered under your
homeowners' or special insurance policy to
cover them under any circumstances.

## 17

Invitations and All Things in Print

Your wedding invitation is the golden ticket to your wedding day.

Think about what you want your beautiful invitations to look like, what they'll convey as far as the formality and style of your wedding, the season, or a theme.

GETTING IDEAS

The sky *is* the limit when it comes to choosing a unique invitation style, with your own personalities reflected in it.

Get a feel for what's going on in the world of wedding invitations by...

- Going to a card or stationery shop and opening up those big, gigantic books filled with sample wedding invitations and announcements. You'll get to touch and feel them, really see how that pearlized border catches the light, feel the raised letters of engraved invitations.
- Visiting invitation websites—such as www.invitations4sale.com, and others you'll find through

bridal websites—and checking out enlarged, detailed graphics of the cards.

- Sending away for sample wedding invitations from companies that send you print versions at your request.
- Looking through bridal magazines.
- Looking through samples at custom stationers' stores.

Once you've checked out the wide range of possibilities, narrow down your choices in style:

__Formal, ecru card with black lettering

__Contemporary formal, such as an ecru card with colored lettering

__Pastel card with black ink

__Pastel card with colored ink

__Bright card with silver or other metallic ink

__Classic card with no border

__Classic card with pearlized or graphic border

__Add your own graphic to the front of the card

__Informal, even humorous, invitation

Your next choices are in design:

__Single-panel card

__Dual-fold (like a traditional greeting card)

__Tri-fold

__Scroll

__Origami style, in which the card is folded to look like a heart or other design, then opens up to reveal your invitation print

___Other:

___White

___Off-white/ecru

___Pastel (pink, light blue, yellow, sage green, etc.
—record your color here):

___Bright (red, green, orange, etc.
—record your color here):

___Other:

Color of Print:

___Black

___Red

___Cranberry

___Hunter green

___Blue

___Purple

___Metallic (silver, gold, copper):

___Other:

Graphics on Your Invitations

Your beach invitation might show seashells, or
starfish, lighthouses, or a sunset over the ocean.
Your autumn wedding invitation might feature colorful fall leaves or acorns, even a pumpkin. Your
winter wedding might show snowflakes. Record your
own wished-for wedding theme graphics—or simply
favorites like roses or gardenias—here:

Raised Print

The process by which your invitations will be created makes a big impact. So consider which process you want:

___Engraved

___Thermography (Looks just like engraved, only letters aren't raised, and there are no engraved-only telltale indentation marks on the back of the invitation. This is the most popular format for invitations today.)

___Letterpress (Growing in popularity today, an elegant non-raised style.)

___Calligraphy

___Home computer printed (Using a font that *looks* like painstaking calligraphy.)

All the Information You Need...

Make sure *all* the important information is included on your wedding invitation:

✓ Your full names

___Your titles (such as Doctor, Lieutenant, etc.)

✓ The names of parents hosting the wedding (All spelled correctly! A typo is *not* the way to start off your relationship with your future in-laws!)

✓ The wedding date

✓ The start time of the ceremony

✓ The location of the ceremony, including street address, town, and state

___Wardrobe indication, stated as "Black Tie Requested" or "Black Tie" (The former meaning,

"We'd like you to wear a tux;" the latter meaning "You *will* wear a tux.")

✓ Reception time and location, including street address—*only* if all of your guests will be invited to the reception. (If not, you'll print up a reception card to be placed in the invitation envelope.)

✓ RSVP date (Listed on the invitation for informal weddings, on the response card in most cases. Set the date early to give yourself plenty of time.)

That's it. Those are the main categories of information that go on the invitation itself. You will then cover the other essentials on separate cards:

✓ Reception card, including the time the reception starts, the name of the reception site, its street address, and any additional notes. (On informal invitations, you might make a note that guests should be ready for a party at the beach, so "bring your sunscreen!")

✓ Response card, which guests will use to indicate how many of them will attend, and which entrée choice they want.

__ At-home card, featuring your address, phone, and perhaps your name change for after the wedding.

✓ Hotel information card, featuring the names and contact numbers of the hotels where guests can get their rooms, block discount code numbers, and even the websites guests can check.

How to Get There

It's a great idea to include maps or written driving directions to your ceremony and reception sites in your invitation packets. Check the following sources to get or make these directions:

- ✓ The ceremony and reception sites themselves will likely offer you packets of pre-printed driving directions from all major highways and directions in the area.
- ___ The ceremony and reception sites' website home page links to driving directions (just print them out.)
- ___ Driving direction sites like www.mapquest.com. You can write them out yourselves, including landmarks.
- ___ Have an artist friend create maps for you as your wedding gift.

Additional Things to Print

You could order them from the invitation printer, or make them yourselves on your home computer. Here's the lineup for your to-do list:

- ✓ Save the Date cards (To be sent out months before the wedding, letting guests know...well, to save the date for your event.)
- ✓ Place cards for guest seating
- ✓ Table number cards
- ___ Menu cards for guest tables
- ___ Dish ID cards for buffet table
- ___ Directional signs (As in, "This way to Doug and Kristina's wedding.")
- ___ Favor tags or labels
- ___ Personalized CD labels, if giving CDs as favors or gifts
- ___ Song request cards for the DJ or band, with a stack placed at every guest table
- ___ Wedding weekend itineraries for guests
- ___ Extra copies of driving directions to wedding sites (Great to give out after the ceremony, in case guests have forgotten theirs!)
- ___ Add your list...

YOUR INVITATION PACKET ASSEMBLY PROCESS

You'll need help putting those invitation packets together, addressing both inside and outside envelopes, *taking one complete invitation packet to the post office to weigh it and get the correct postage due for each,* buy stamps, seal the envelopes, and get them out on time.

So list your invitation packet helpers and the job each will do to help. (Note: provide lunch or dinner for your helpers…it's going to be a long process!)

Pre-Assembly Musts

- Make sure you have the correct spelling of all of your guests' names, and their titles (such as Doctor, Captain, etc.).
- Make sure you have the current addresses for all of your guests.
- Make sure you have the correct number and names of guests' kids, if kids are invited.
- Make sure you send the invitations out early; 6 to 8 weeks in advance is the norm, 12 to 14 weeks for a destination wedding.
- Have a system for handling RSVPs.
- Make sure your hands are clean! No smudges on fresh envelopes.
- No liquid paper! If you make a mistake, start over on a fresh envelope.
- Assign someone with great handwriting to do the addresses.
- Switch jobs from time to time to prevent monotony and mistakes.
- Take breaks. Have a drink.
- Make it fun!

___Take one assembled packet to the post office for weighing

___Buy "Love" or theme postage stamps

___Buy calligraphy or specialty pens

___Address outside envelopes

___Add names to inside envelopes

___Assemble invitations together with inserts and tissue papers

___Affix the stamps to the outer envelopes

___Affix the stamps to the response cards

___Seal the envelopes

___Double-check invitations against master guest list to make sure no one was left out

___Affix return address labels, if necessary

___Put wax seal, monogram label or other adornment on outside envelope

___Other:

YOUR WEDDING PROGRAM

These programs will be handed out at your ceremony, so that everyone in attendance knows what's going on, what's coming up, and who's who.

Here are the categories you should include in your program:

___A beautiful cover page, perhaps with a bridal-appropriate graphic or a picture of the two of you, with your names and your wedding date

___A welcome message from the two of you

___A poem or quote you love, emphasizing the meaning of the day for you

___The names and titles of everyone in your wedding party

___All parents' names

___Grandparents' names, if you wish to include them

___The officiant's name

___The schedule of your ceremony, from processional to readings to vows to ring exchange to recessional

___The names of everyone performing readings, plus the names of the readings

___The names of everyone performing the songs, plus the names of the songs

___The titles of songs played during your ceremony, together with the composers' names

___Explanations of any ethnic, cultural, or religious rituals, so that guests can follow along

___A copy of your vow wording, if you wish

___A thank you note from the two of you, thanking all those who helped plan the wedding

___A note of tribute in the memory of departed loved ones. Some couples write that their floral arrangements are in memory of (insert name, name, and name)

___Another poem or quote that reflects your going onward into a beautiful future together

___Your "at home" information, including your name change, if applicable

___Perhaps a small graphic of the two of you on the back cover

___Your additional ideas:

# of programs needed:

# of program covers needed:

# of ribbon ties or tassels needed to secure programs:

Office copy shop order #:

Price:

Payment due:

Who's handing the programs out at the wedding:

18

Your Flowers

This checklist chapter helps you make the first, essential decisions so that you can approach your florist with a clear picture of your floral wishes, ready to bring each choice to life.

First Thing's First: Color

The Bride's Bouquet:

___All white

___All pastel, monochromatic

___All pastel, mixed range of colors

___All brights, monochromatic (like an all lipstick-red bouquet)

✓ All brights, mixed range of colors

___White and pastel

___White and brights

___All cream-colored (to match a cream-colored gown)

___Cream and pastel

___Cream and brights

Your Bridesmaids' Bouquets:

___All white (A trendy new look: the bridesmaids get the white bouquet, while you get the bright one.)

___All pastel, monochromatic

___All pastel, mixed range of colors

___All brights, monochromatic (like an all lipstick-red bouquet)

_✓_All brights, mixed range of colors

___White and pastel

___White and brights

___All cream-colored (to match a cream-colored gown)

___Cream and pastel

___Cream and brights

___Your Maid of Honor's bouquet color (if set apart):

The Mothers'/Grandmothers'/Godmothers' Corsages or Nosegay Bouquets:

___All white

___All pastel, monochromatic

___All pastel, mixed range of colors

___All brights, monochromatic (like an all lipstick-red bouquet)

_✓_All brights, mixed range of colors

___White and pastel

___White and brights

___All cream-colored (to match a cream-colored gown)

___Cream and pastel

___Cream and brights

___Color to match/coordinate with her dress:

The Flower Girls' Rose Petals, Floral Wreath, or Nosegay Colors:

__Whites
__Pastels
✓Brights
__Color mix:

The Men's Boutonnieres:

__White
__Cream
__Pastel
✓Bright
__Color chosen:
__Groom and best man's boutonniere color to set them apart:
__Fathers'/grandfathers'/stepfathers'/godfathers' color to set them apart:

Your Color Worksheet

Write down the color mixes you love for your maids' gowns and flowers, which feed directly into the color scheme for your entire wedding. Check out www.bliss-weddings.com for their fun, interactive flower color/dress coordination chart with graphics to view. Present these ideas to your florist to see the amazing and unique combinations he or she can create for you:

-
-
-
-

Sizes of Your Bouquets and Floralwear

The Bride's Bouquet:

___Small

_✓_Medium

___Large

___Cascading

_✓_Hand-tied (traditional round style)

___Long-stems tied with ribbon at base

___Other:

The Bridesmaids' Bouquets:

_✓_Small

___Medium

___Large

___Cascading

_✓_Hand-tied (traditional round style)

___Long-stems tied with ribbon at base

___Other:

The Mothers' and Others' Flowers:

_✓_Corsage, small

___Corsage, medium

_✓_Wrist corsage

___Bouquet, small

___Bouquet, medium

___Floral bracelet

___Floral necklace/choker

___Other:

Who Gets the Rose?

List here the names of your mothers, stepmothers, grandmothers, godmothers, and anyone else who will receive a corsage or floralwear piece:

-
-
-
-
-
-
-
-
-
-

The Flower Girl Flowers:

__Floral wreath for hair

✓Wrist corsage

__Bouquet, small

__Bouquet, medium

__Pomander

__Floral bracelet

__Floral necklace/choker

__None

__Other:

The Men's Boutonnieres:

__Small, single-flower

✓Medium, single-flower

__Spray

__Other:

How Many Will You Need?

List here all the men who will receive a boutonniere, including the wedding party, fathers, grandfathers, stepfathers, godfathers, etc:

-
-
-
-
-
-
-
-
-
-
-
-

Centerpieces:

__Small, low-set

__Medium

__Large

__Extra-large

__Petals only, to surround candles

__Single flower floating in vase

__Other:

__How many will you need?

Picking Flowers

While I have some of the most popular wedding flower varieties listed here to get you started, visit floral websites and www.blissweddings.com's flower generator tool to pick out the lovely blooms you want for your wedding day bouquets and centerpieces:

Your Chosen Flower Types:

Roses
Gardenias
Stephanotis
Lilies
Peonies
Daisies
Calla lilies
Gerbera daisies
Sunflowers
Tulips
Ranunculus
Other:

Fillers and Greenery:

Baby's breath
Queen Anne's lace
Fern
Ivy
Flowering branches (for centerpieces)
Fruits, nuts, figs, and other unique elements
Other:

Going Green

Greenery is fast becoming one of the top ways to give a natural, lush look to centerpieces and bouquets, and florists are filling the need with great advice on unique greenery that gives your arrangements an extra special look. Ask to see the wide range of possibilities.

Your chosen bouquet elements:
Your chosen centerpiece elements:

Flowers for the Boutonnieres:

__Rose
__Stephanotis
__Orchid
__Other:
__Groom and Best Man type of flower:
__All other men's type of flower:

Your Centerpiece Dreams:

__Oversized, cascading, elevated above the table on stands or in candelabra holders
__Oversized, but sitting low on the table
__Low clusters of tight floral bunches in vases
__A single floating flower (like a gardenia) in a water-filled bowl
__Several floating flowers, like gardenias or bright Gerbera daisies, floating in a water-filled bowl
__Rose petals sprinkled around pillar candles on a platter
__Rose petals in a clear vase

___Fruit piles with floral inserts (like a pile of lemons to suit your yellow theme, with stephanotis sprigs tucked in)

___Non-floral: bread basket, framed photos, top hats, etc.

___Other:

All Matching Centerpieces

___All centerpieces will match

___Smaller centerpieces for the cake table, guest book table, gift table, and family picture table

___Centerpiece style will be used for altar arrangement

___Your plans for additional arrangements, size, style, etc.

Your centerpiece plans:

Your chosen tribute floral arrangement plans:

Flowers to top the cake:

ADDITIONAL HELP FROM THE FLORIST

Your florist can be your one-stop source for the following:

___Chuppah rental or creation

___Aisle runner

___Chair slipcovers

___Décor fabric

___Trellis

___Rented potted trees for décor

___Lighting contacts

___Getaway car décor

___Thank you bouquets or arrangements delivered
to your parents on the morning after the wedding

19

Limousines and Other Transportation

Making the right choices means feeling like a true celebrity on your day, and having *terrific* pictures of your big arrival.

First, what kind of car do you want?

___Limousine, white

___Limousine, black (Photographers tell me that the black limo is a top choice, since it contrasts so well with the bride's white or off-white gown.)

___Classic or luxury car:

Rolls Royce	Convertible
Bentley	Aston Martin
Excalibur	Other:

___Stretch Humvee or Navigator

✓Other

Creative Choices

They're not cars, but you can rent them for an extra special arrival or departure…

__Trolley

__Sleigh

__Horse and carriage

__Snowmobile

__Yacht or boat

__Yellow cab

And of course, you might find that you *don't* have to rent a car or other transportation at all! If your ceremony and reception take place in the same location—such as at a hotel ballroom or outdoor gardens—no rides are needed. And then of course, you always have the option of using cars at your disposal for free:

__Your own car, decorated with streamers or cling-on "Just Married" signs

__A friend's or relative's gleaming car or convertible

__A friend's or relative's prized classic car

FINDING A GREAT CAR COMPANY

The beauty of the car is one thing, but the company's reliability is of the utmost importance. Finding the *best* car company out there is essential, so that your ride shows up on time and gets you there safely. Here's where you'll start your search:

- Referrals from recently married friends and family
- Classic car clubs (search online)

- Your state's car association (search online)
- Recommendations from your wedding coordinator
- Bridal expos and showcases
- Classic car shows. You'll see these advertised in the paper, hosted by auto dealers, hotels, even cigar bars and sports bars. Spend a fun afternoon checking out all the antique and classic cars and ask the owners if they rent out for weddings. Some owners consider their cars their "babies" and never sell their time. But others make a fine side living from their investment, working weddings on the weekends.

How Many Cars Will You Need?

You can find limousines that seat anywhere from eight to fourteen people. Stretch specialty cars might hold twenty or so people. At this point, you need to decide who will get rides in your rented luxury cars on the wedding day—such as the bridesmaids and groomsmen, the parents and grandparents, siblings, and their dates, *you*—and from there configure the number of cars you'll need to rent.

Inspecting the Cars Yourselves

Always, always, always make sure you get to check out the cars yourselves. A quality company will let you inspect the cars inside and out. Here's what you're looking for:

- The age of the car
- That it's well-maintained (Cars should be washed and waxed)
- A clean interior with no ripped seats, stains, or odors
- Working parts—the interior lights work, the privacy window works, the radio works
- Plenty of room for you to fit your gown lengths
- The extras you want: An ice compartment, champagne glass holders, mood lighting, etc.

ADDITIONAL RIDES NEEDED

Throughout the wedding weekend, you or others (like wedding guests and wedding party members) might need a pickup or drop-off. Here is where you'll organize who has volunteered to do any needed driving, such as picking up select guests from the airport:

Volunteer #1:

Volunteer #2:

Volunteer #3:

Volunteer #4:

Or you could arrange for the following transportation help:

___Free use of the hotel's shuttle bus for your guests

___Free use of the hotel's limousine or car service for your guests

___The name and number of a taxicab company:

Assorted Details

Just a few extra details regarding transportation that you need to check on at both your ceremony and reception sites, and also at home if you'll host any pre- or post-wedding events:

__Is there valet parking available?

__Can you negotiate for free valet service?

__Where can you hire a valet service company?

__Do you need parking permits?

__Can you arrange for free parking at the hotel for your guests? (Some hotels charge a nightly fee for guest parking.)

__Do you have room for parking at your home?

__Do you need to get permits for overnight parking at your home? (Important! Check with your town police department for overnight parking permits if you live in a neighborhood where ticketing could happen—some of your guests might need to stay at your place, and some police departments consider cars on the street after 2 a.m. to be considered "overnight"—even if it's New Year's Eve!)

20

Photography

In this section, you'll plan out your photo wish list, and find the most talented expert to take those pictures on your big day.

Your Wedding Day Photo Wish List

(Note: hand this list to your photographer, with the shots you want indicated with a ✓ and the ones you *don't* want given an **X**)

Getting Ready for the Big Day

✓ Bride in pre-wedding casual attire, holding a mug of coffee with her engagement-ring only (so far!) hand

___ Bride on the phone with the groom

✓ Bride's gown hanging in the bedroom, before the bride steps into it

✓ Bridesmaids' arrival, hugs with the bride

✓ Bridal breakfast, including a champagne toast

✓ Bride and her entourage going to the beauty salon

✓ Bride and her entourage returning from the beauty salon (as in "before" and "after" shots)

✓ Bride and bridesmaids getting ready for the wedding

☑ Mom or Maid of Honor helping bride attach her veil

☑ Dad's first look at the bride in her wedding gown

☑ Full-length shot of bride in her gown, from several angles, in several settings

☑ Bride and her maids, fully dressed, having a champagne toast or posing out in the garden

___Bride and her parents

___Bride with her sisters or siblings

___Bride being given her something old, something new, something borrowed, something blue

___Bride's first look at her wedding bouquet as she unwraps the box

___Bride holding her bouquet

___Bride with her grandparents

___Bride with her mother

___Bride with her mother and grandmother(s)

___Bride with her stepmother

___Bride with her mother and stepmother

___Bride with her father

___Bride with her stepfather

___Bride with her father and stepfather

___Bride with her godmother and godfather

___Bride with her parents and stepparents

___Bride with her Maid or Matron of Honor

___Bride with her bridesmaids, formal pose

___Bride with her bridesmaids, casual pose

___Bride with flower girls

___Bride with each of her bridesmaids, individually

___Bride and bridesmaids departing for the ceremony, posing in front of the limo or waving from the window as the car pulls away

___Groom in casual attire, hanging out with his buddies before the wedding
___Groom getting ready for the wedding
___Groom getting help with his tie
___Groomsmen getting ready
___Best Man hugging the groom or shaking hands with the groom
___Groom with his parents and/or stepparents
___Groom with his father
___Groom with his stepfather
___Groom with his father and stepfather
___Groom with his mother
___Groom with his stepmother
___Groom with his mother and stepmother
___Groom with his godparents
___Groom with his siblings
___Groom with his groomsmen
___Groom and groomsmen putting on their boutonnieres
___Groom getting a high-five from the ringbearer
___Groom and his men departing for the ceremony
___Groom arriving at the ceremony site
___Groom and his men in the waiting room at the ceremony site

___Bride and her parents en route to the ceremony (in the limousine, looking out the window as the

car or carriage makes its way to the site)
___Bride arriving at the ceremony site
___Father or parents helping the bride out of the car
___Bride and wedding party taking their places to await the start of the ceremony
___Maid of Honor adjusting the bride's train or veil before the ceremony starts
___Wink from father, or from bride to father/parents, before the processional starts

At the Ceremony

___Pictures of the ceremony site exterior
___A picture of the empty, decorated ceremony site before guests arrive
___A wide-angle shot of the ceremony site from a balcony as the guest arrive
___Guests arriving and being seated
___Special guests arriving and being escorted to their seats
___Ushers escorting mothers to their seats (Christian wedding)
___Groom and groomsmen taking their place at the altar
___Bridesmaids walking down the aisle
___Flower girl and/or ring bearer walking down the aisle
___Maid of Honor walking down the aisle
___Bride's first appearance at the end of the aisle
___Bride and her parents walking down the aisle
___A close-up of the groom's face when he first sees

his bride

___A clasp of the bride's face when she first sees her groom

___Bride and parents meeting with the groom at the altar

___The groom and the bride's father shaking hands before the presentation of the bride to the groom

___Bride and groom taking hands at the altar

___Wide-angle shot from the balcony capturing the moment the bride and groom take their places at the altar, including the guests in their seats

___Bride and groom kneeling at the altar OR circling the altar in traditional custom

___Bride and groom listening to the officiant speak

___Readings and musical performances

___Mothers lighting the unity candle

___Bride and groom lighting the unity candle

___Bride and groom greeting their parents and offering peace as part of the ceremony

___Any religious or cultural rituals performed for the ceremony

___Bride and groom exchanging vows

___Bride and groom exchanging rings

___Close-up of bride's and groom's hands as they place the rings on each other's fingers

___Bride and groom's first kiss as husband and wife

___Bride and groom turn to their applauding audience

___Bride and groom jumping the broom, if an African American ceremony

___Bride and groom walk back down the aisle

___Bride and groom exit ceremony site and kiss

___Recessional to capture wedding party, parents, and guests greeting the couple at the exit of the ceremony site

___The receiving line

___The shower of birdseed or bubbles as the couple runs to the limousine

___Bride and groom leaving ceremony site with a "Just Married" sign on the back of the car

___Bride and groom standing up out of the limousine sunroof waving goodbye

___Bride and groom in limousine backseat

Post–Ceremony Photos

___Bride and groom embracing

___Bride and groom sealed in a kiss

___Bride and groom with the bride's parents

___Bride and groom with the groom's parents

___Bride and groom with both sets of parents

___Bride and groom with both sets of parents and both sets of grandparents

___Bride and groom with her grandparents

___Bride and groom with his grandparents

___Bride and groom individually with each of their grandparents

___Bride and groom with bride's extended family

___Bride and groom with groom's extended family

___Bride and groom with all family members

___Bride and groom with all wedding guests

___Bride, groom, and all of their siblings

___Bride and groom with bridesmaids

___Bride and groom with Maid of Honor

___Bride and groom with all female attendants

___Bride and groom with Best Man

___Bride and groom with all groomsmen

___Bride and groom with child attendants

___Bride and groom with entire wedding party

At the Reception

___Photos of the reception site outside

___Photos of scenery around the reception site, like the sunset or a lit fountain

___Photos of empty, decorated reception room while everyone's in the cocktail hour room

___Sweetheart's table decorated for the bride and groom

___The family photo table, featuring framed pictures of relatives and friends

___Random shots of guests at the cocktail hour and beginning of reception

___Parents and wedding party being introduced into the room

___Bride and groom arriving at the reception site

___Bride and groom making their way to the ballroom

___Bride and groom making their grand entrance into the ballroom

___Bride and groom during their first dance

___Bride dancing with her father

___Groom dancing with his mother

___First full dance of the evening; wedding party members and guests dancing with one another

___Bride and groom dancing with the flower girls or ringbearer

___Best Man's toast

___Maid of Honor's toast

___Parents' toast

___Couple's toast

___Bride and groom toasting one another

___Close-up of the bride and groom's toasting flutes clinking together

___Parents dancing

___Bride dancing with the bridesmaids

___Bride dancing with grandparents

___Kids dancing or playing

___Entertainers performing

___Guests partying

___The cake

___Bride and groom cutting the cake

___Bride and groom feeding each other pieces of cake

___The bouquet toss

___The woman catching the bouquet

___The bride congratulating her

___Removal and tossing of the garter

___Candid shots from the evening

___Requested group shots

___Bride and groom leaving the reception, saying goodbye to special guests

___Scenes from the after-party

___Your additional photo wish list

(Ask specifically for shots like "Bride dancing with great-uncle, Bride with grandmother and her sisters," etc.)

-
-
-
-
-
-
-
-
-
-
-
-

FINDING YOUR PHOTOGRAPHER

The key is to find a terrific photographer, one who listens to your requests and wishes and is able to produce the kinds of shots you want for your day.

Here is where you'll start your search—and start it as early as possible!—for the expert you'll entrust with your most important pictures from the day:

___Recommendations from recently-married friends and family

___Recommendations from your wedding coordinator

___Interviewing off the list of member photographers at a professional association (search online for your regional association chapter)

___Interviewing photographers you meet at bridal shows and expos

___Online search through photographers' Webster, after seeing their samples

WHO GETS THEIR OWN PHOTO ALBUMS?

Here's where you'll record who you'll buy albums (or DVDs) for: (Don't forget that you can *make* albums from your proofs or from candid shots others have taken.)

___Extra album for you

___Bride's parents (put number of copies needed in case you have mother and father living apart, perhaps remarried)

___Groom's parents (put number of copies in case more than one is needed)

___Bride's grandparents

___Groom's grandparents

___Maid of Honor

___Best Man

___Bridesmaids

___Groomsmen

___Parents of the flower girls

___Parents of the ringbearer

___Godparents

___Others:

# of albums needed:

Plans for labeling the albums (as in, you'll make them, you'll order engraved plates to attach to them, you'll order online):

the busy bride's essential wedding checklists

## 21

Videography

If you're like most couples, you see the value in capturing your wedding day on videotape shot by a professional. Even at a lofty expense, it's worth it to have expert footage of an unforgettable day, and your tape or DVD only grows more valuable to you over time.

YOUR VIDEO PREFERENCES

You can save time and get just what you want by making the following selection, showing these pages to your chosen videographer:

Would You Like That Raw?

A "raw tape" is one that hasn't been edited at all. The videographer just shoots the footage as it happens and then hands the tape to you. No fancy editing. No bringing the footage down to just one hour of time. No expensive special effects added. Some couples choose this option for now, with plans to have their wedding day footage edited in the future when they can better afford an expert treatment. This is often a great first anniversary gift the couple invests in.

___Raw tape

___Lightly edited tape

___Heavily edited tape

___Special effects:

___Childhood photo montage

___Soundtrack

___Interviews with the two of you

___Interviews with family

___Slow motion

___Pull focus

___Black and white

___Other: (check with videographer to see what's possible)

You also can have your choice of whether you want one-camera footage or more than one. By that, I mean your wedding (especially your ceremony) is shot with two or more different cameras from different angles, so that the editor can expertly weave together close-ups of the two of you plus long shots from, say, the balcony. Using more than one camera and requiring extra editing will cost you, but it often gives that professional documentary look that really captures your day.

You Want:

___1 camera

___2 cameras

___3 cameras

Which Format?

___VHS

__DVD
__Both

Which Events Will the Pro Shoot?

Most couples hire their videographer only for the entirety of the wedding day, from ceremony start to reception finish. But others bring in a professional to shoot expert footage from additional events. You can hire the pro for these, or ask a friend to bring along his or her own camcorder:

The Basics:

__Wedding morning

__Getting ready

__Posing for pictures

__The ceremony

__Post-ceremony

__The reception

Add-Ons:

__The engagement party

__The bride's first time trying on her gown

__The bride's final fitting

__The men getting their tuxes

__Wedding weekend activities

__The rehearsal

__The rehearsal dinner

__The after-party

__The morning-after breakfast

__Other events:

-
-

-
-
-

Your Personalized Montage

If your wedding videotape will open with pictures of the two of you as babies and throughout your "growing up" years and courtship, here's where you'll plan out the pictures you'll submit to your videographer:

-
-
-
-
-
-
-

And now list the songs you'd like used as the backdrop for your montage and throughout the wedding videotape, including "your song" and any other music that is special to you. (You can provide the videographer with a CD of these songs for easy use on your project.)

Example: "At Last" by Etta James

-
-
-
-
-
-

Your Footage Wish List

Check back to your photographers' shot list for ideas on wedding day footage that you definitely want. Your video expert knows which obvious footage to get, but you'll likely want to brief him or her on any special moments you want captured on film forever.

___You and your siblings spending some time together on the morning of the wedding

___The groom and his guys playing a round of golf on the morning of the wedding

___Your morning phone call to the groom for a last-minute "I Love You" before the ceremony

___You and the groom in the limousine right after the ceremony—capturing your first breathless comments to each other

___A special girls-only toast at the bar with all of your best friends raising a drink to you

___You dancing with your favorite great-uncle

___The flower girls and ringbearer playing or dancing at the reception

___You holding your sister's new baby

___Your parents dancing with one another

___Your grandparents dancing with one another

___Now you create your own special shots list:

Who Gets a Copy?

Rather than duplicating copies of your own master wedding videotape, which can damage it, you'll order extra copies from your videographer. Here is where you'll check off who gets their own copy of the tape or DVD, and how many you'll need:

___Extra copy for you

___Bride's parents (put number of copies needed in case you have mother and father living apart, perhaps remarried)

___Groom's parents (put number of copies in case more than one is needed)

___Bride's grandparents

___Groom's grandparents

___Maid of Honor

___Best Man

___Bridesmaids

___Groomsmen

___Parents of the flower girls

___Parents of the ringbearer

___Godparents

___Others:

# of tape cases needed:

Plans for labeling the videotape or DVD: (as in, videographer makes them, you'll make them, you'll order engraved plates to attach to them, you'll order online)

Part Six

Planning Your Reception

## 22

What You Need to Rent

You may find that your site doesn't supply all the items you'll need, and that you'll have to rent some essentials. In this section, you'll check off the items on your rental-shopping list. (Hint: Get some advice from your site manager, wedding coordinator, or rental specialist—you'll undoubtedly hear about items you didn't know you needed!)

Finding a Rental Agent

Check at www.ararental.org to find a quality rental agency near you.

__Tents
__Tables (different sizes available!)
__Chairs
__Table linens
__Chair linens
__Dishes and chargers—complete china sets
__Silverware
__Stemware—champagne and wine glasses
__Drinking glasses—mixed drink, martini, etc.

___Serving utensils

___Tent liners

___Tent support anchors

___Table skirts

___Arches or trellises

___Chuppah

___Aisle runner

___Display pedestals

___Centerpieces

___Plant stands

___Dance floors

___Portable bars

___Chafing dishes

___Champagne fountains

___Wine fountains

___Chocolate fountains

___Fondue sets

___Cooking equipment

___Coolers

___Grills

___Sound systems

___Lighting systems

___Fountains

___Coffeemakers

___Espresso makers

___Cappuccino makers

___Coffee cups and saucers

___Pitchers

___Trays

___Canopies

___Walkways

___Footbridges

___Audiovisual display machines

___Heat lamps

___Warming trays

___Musician equipment and stands

___Games and inflatables for kids

___Popcorn machines

___Cotton candy machines

___Ice cream machines

___International coffee dispenser machines

___Bubble machines

___Snowmaking machines

___Décor items

___Portable restrooms

___Candleholders

___Candelabras

___Punch bowls

___Steamers

___Umbrellas

___Ring pillow

___Other:

___Other:

___Other:

___Other:

23

Your Menu

Go unique, go traditional, go trendy, or go ethnic.
You can't go wrong if the choices suit your style of
wedding, your personal preferences, and if the
caterer is truly talented.

FINDING YOUR CATERER

You'll find yourself with the following options:
- Using the site's in-house caterer
- Hiring your own caterer
- And, also, perhaps preparing some dishes on
  your own, or having a relative or friend make
  some specialty dishes

If you're of the first two varieties, there are
choices and interviews involved. Tastings, even, so
that you can sample their talents. It all starts with
finding the best expert possible:

__Interview the site's in-house caterers.

__Ask recently married friends and family for
referrals.

__Check with a professional caterers' organization
(like www.nace.net).

___If you'll have a small wedding, check out personal chefs' associations (like www.uspca.com or www.personalchef.com).

___Check with ethnic or cultural associations to find their specialty chefs and caterers.

___Over time, sample the food choices at restaurants and delis that cater hot and cold foods, party platters, etc.

Your caterer will be:

CATERING YOUR RECEPTION'S STYLE

Before you choose individual dishes, you'll have to figure out how they will be served:

Cocktail Hour: (check all that apply)

___Hot passed hors d'oeuvres

___Cold passed hors d'oeuvres

___Buffet

___Seafood buffet

___Food stations, unmanned

___Food stations, with attendants

___Traveling cocktail hour, with different stations set up throughout your site

___Other:

Dinner Hour: (check all that apply)

___Sit-down dinner, served by waiters

___Sit-down dinner, buffet-style

___Food stations

___Other:

Brunch or Tea?

For afternoon receptions, your chosen style might be a brunch or a tea. Here, you'll check off which serving style you prefer: (check more than one if applicable)

___Sit-down, served

___Buffet

___Food stations

___Passed selections presented on trays by servers

CHICKEN OR BEEF?

You'll choose the details of your menu in just a moment. But first, here is where you'll decide on the main entrée categories (check all that apply, usually 2 to 3 choices offered to your guests):

___Beef

___Chicken

___Fish

___Shellfish (like lobster tails, crab, shrimp, etc.)

___Pasta

___Lamb

___Pork

___Ethnic or theme entrée

___Vegetarian Choice

___Vegan Choice

___Combination Platter (i.e. several shrimp and several beef medallions on each plate)

___Other:

Who's Allergic to Shellfish?

If you know that a family member—or perhaps one of you—is allergic to certain foods, you'll certainly want to keep those food items out of your wedding menu. Here is where you'll record who is allergic to which food items, and then hand this important list to your caterer:

-
-
-
-

CHOOSING MENU ITEMS

You'll of course have the caterer's menu possibilities list in front of you, a lengthy document listing dozens and dozens of appetizer choices ("Pick eight"), fifty ways to prepare chicken ("Pick one? Are you kidding?"), and some dishes you've never heard of before ("What in the world is *that*?"). I've provided some sample ideas in each category. You can highlight those if they interest you, and then go on to write down your favorite choices from the caterer's list:

Hot Passed Hors d'oeuvres
- Phyllo pockets with crabmeat filling
- Mini-meatballs
- Chicken and beef satay skewers

Cold Passed Hors d'oeuvres
- Shrimp cocktail
- Sliced salami or prosciutto
- Crudités

Buffet

- Lemon chicken
- Pasta with marinara sauce
- Cheese platter, with selection of hard and soft cheeses
- Fruit platter

Ice Sculptures

If you'd like an ice sculpture on your buffet table, designate the shape and design here, and share this information with the site manager or your caterer:

Salad

- Mesclun
- Spinach
- Caesar

Soup

- Lobster bisque
- Onion
- New England or Manhattan clam chowder

Food Stations

- Carving station, with prime rib or honey glazed ham
- Pasta station with a variety of pasta shapes and sauces (marinara, alfredo, pesto, etc.)
- Sushi
- Raw seafood bar

Intermezzo

At some weddings, a "refresher course" is served, in the form of a single scoop of sorbet to cleanse the palate before the entrée. Decide which flavor of sorbet you'd prefer:

__Lemon

__Lime

__Orange

__Berry

__Passionfruit

__Flavor swirl

__Other:

Entrée

- Soy-glazed salmon
- Filet mignon
- Chicken marsala
- Beef medallions with sautéed shrimp
- Pork in mushroom glaze

Side Dishes

- Garlic mashed potatoes
- Asparagus tied with rosemary
- Broccoli flowers with Romano cheese
- Sweet potato "straws" (or fries)

Garnishing Plan

A great caterer can garnish your entrees or appetizers with special flair, personalizing your menu to you. Choose from the following:

___Our monogram powder-stenciled onto appetizer items

___Our monogram swirled in sauce

___Sauce heart swirls

___Powdered sugar stencil designs on desserts

___Other:

Additional menu choices:

Our final catering choices:

Catering Worksheet

Company Name:

Chef's name:

Address:

Phone:

Fax:

Cell #:

Hours in package:

Package details:

Additional Rentals:

Permits needed:

Deposit paid:

Delivery date, time, and place:

Full payment due:
Full payment paid:
Additional notes:

## 24

The Wedding Cake

Your first step to an unforgettable, indulgent wedding cake is finding the right baker. Someone with experience and artistry, a fine reputation in the industry, and reliability. Here are your steps:

__You'll of course ask your friends for referrals (the best way to go), but you might also check through wedding experts for the best candidates.

__You'll schedule an interview and tour the baker's workshop, sitting down for a tasting of his or her samples in order to make your final decision, and talk about customizing your wedding cake flavors and design. A great baker can do whatever you wish.

__Together, you'll figure out the correct size of cake needed for your guest head count.

__You'll decide on the shape, number of tiers, and your chosen flavors and décor (see checklists in this chapter to help you decide).

__You'll discuss the payment and delivery terms with your baker, filling in the details on this worksheet:

Circle those that interest you, so that you can let your baker know best how to please you...

Cake Flavors:

Yellow	Chocolate
Vanilla	Chocolate ganache
Vanilla cream	Chocolate chip
Lemon	White
Carrot	Butter
Orange	Fudge marble
Angel food	Almond hazelnut
Spice	Marble pound
Almond chiffon	Devil's food
Coconut	Espresso
Others:	

Fillings:

Buttercream	Lemon
Berry	Chocolate mousse
Cherry	Strawberry
Blueberry	Raspberry
Passionfruit	Cannoli cream
Vanilla crème	Cream cheese
Apple cinnamon	Lemon cream
Chocolate truffle	Mango mousse
Ginger cream	White chocolate buttercream
Coconut cream	Lemon curd
Vanilla bavarian	Custard
Ice cream	Cheesecake
Macadamia mousse	Banana mousse
Hazelnut mousse	Others:

Frostings:

Buttercream	Rolled fondant
Mocha buttercream	Strawberry cream
Cream cheese	Chocolate
White chocolate	Lemon cream
Icing with coconut	Sugar paste icing
Royal icing	Marzipan
Others:	

Coffee and Liquor Soaks:

Rum	Espresso
Cappuccino	Grand Marnier
Kahlúa	Frangelico
Others:	

Sauces for Your Cake:

Raspberry	Lemon
Strawberry	Chocolate
Vanilla	Cherry
Caramel	Espresso
Others:	

Cake Toppers

What will stand atop your cake?

___Traditional mini bride and groom

___A cascade of fresh flowers

___A crystal figurine

___A tiara surrounded by fresh flowers

___A silk flower arrangement

___Seashells

___Other:

Cake topper store:

Who's buying the cake topper?

Weight of the cake topper (for the baker's information):

GROOM'S CAKE

If you'll have a separate cake in addition to the wedding cake—known as the Groom's Cake, and often in a decadent, rich flavor, styled in a unique theme shape—use the checklist ideas above to plan the makings of your own second confection.

Groom's Cake Shape/Theme:

Groom's Cake Flavor:

Groom's Cake Filling:

Groom's Cake Icing:

Baker:

Payment Due:

Delivery Instructions:

ADDITIONAL DESSERTS TO CONSIDER:

Chocolate-covered strawberries

Bananas foster

Truffles and chocolates

Chocolate mousse

Ice cream

Cheesecake

Petits fours

Carrot cake

Pastries

Iced cupcakes

Strawberries with
whipped cream

Chocolate fondue

Pies (apple, cherry,
blueberry, etc.)

Angel food cake

Decorated cookies

Raspberries with
whipped cream

Tropical fruits

Others:

Additional desserts chosen:

## 25

Stocking the Bar

Your bar menu adds some excitement to the celebration and gives your guests something terrific to toast you with. So as you work with your bar manager—or on your own if you're self-catering—think about the following drinks available at your bar:

Go to the Source

To find the perfect vintages, read about wine ratings and awards, and learn about pairing wines with foods, visit www.winespectator.com.

Fine Champagne:

__Champagne with strawberries or raspberries at the bottom of each flute

__Champagne "dressed up" with splashes of fruit juice

__Red wines

__White wines

__Blush wines

Classic Mixed Drinks:

__Jack and Coke

__Rum and Coke

__Gin and tonic

___Vodka tonic

___Scotch and soda

___White Russian

___Sidecar

___Bay Breeze

___Fuzzy Navel

___Screwdriver

___Rusty Nail

Martini Bar:

___Cosmopolitan

___Appletini

___Chocolate martini

___Key lime martini

___Pear martini

___Espresso martini

___Tiffany blue martini

___Lemon drop martini

___Other (check out www.foodtv.com for martini recipes):

Party Drinks:

___Mojito

___Bellini

___Piña colada

___Daiquiri

___Margarita

___Mudslide

___Flirtini (raspberry, lime, pineapple, and cranberry flavored)

___Sangria

___Other (go to your favorite bar and ask the bar-
tender what's hot right now):

Hard Liquors to Stock Your Bar:

___Vodka	___Scotch	___Tequila
___Gin	___Sweet	___Port
___Dry vermouth	vermouth	___Kahlúa
___Brandy	___Cognac	___Other:
___Bourbon	___Whiskey	

Beer:

___Light beer	___Lager	___Ale
___Low carb beer	___Stoudt	___Cider beer
___Domestic beer	___Microbrew	___Imported beer
___Seasonal	___Other:	

Mixers and Non-Alcoholic Drink Menu:

___Cola	___Diet cola	___Cranberry
___Orange juice	___Pineapple	juice
___Sour mix	juice	___Lemon-lime
___Bottled water	___Sparkling	___Tonic water
___Diet cola	water	___Iced tea
___Lemonade	___Fruit Punch	___Soda water
___Milk	___Heavy cream	___Other:

Hot Drinks:

__Coffee, regular
__Cappuccino
__Tea
__Herbal tea
__Spiced rum

__Coffee, decaf
__Jamaican
    coffee
__Hot chocolate
__Other:

__Espresso
__Irish coffee
__Chai tea
__Spiced cider

After Dinner Drinks:

__Bailey's Irish
    Cream
__Sambuca
__Frangelico

__Grand
    Marnier
__Brandy
__Chambord

__Amaretto
__Cognac
__Other:

Stock Up for Your Bar:

__Ice cubes
__Orange
    wedges
__Drink stirrers
__Coasters
__Worcester-
    shire sauce

__Lemon
    wedges
__Maraschino
    cherries
__Olives
__Tabasco sauce
__Lime wedges

__Salt (for rims)
__Lime juice
__Straws
__Other:

## 26

Décor and Place Settings

Call this a catchall chapter, where you'll list your own personalized ideas:

Table Settings:

China pattern to be used at cocktail hour:
needed:

China pattern to be used at dinner hour:
needed:

China pattern for dessert hour:
needed:

Stemware pattern for wedding event:

__Champagne flutes
__Red wine glasses
__White wine glasses
__Martini glasses
__Highballs
__Tumblers
__Martini glasses
__Margarita glasses

___Other:

needed: (fill in above)
Flatware pattern for wedding event:
needed

Serving platters and serveware:
needed:

Table Linens:
___Table linens for cocktail party
___Table linens for reception
___Linens for cake table
___Linens for gift table
___Linens for guest book table
___Other linens:
needed:

Check with the Experts

Ask your wedding coordinator, site and bar managers what else you might need that they haven't provided. Very often, what seems like common sense to them might not even occur to you. (After all, you haven't planned many weddings!) One wedding coordinator tells me that she encouraged a couple holding an outdoor wedding to rent colorful umbrellas for their guests at $2 a pop. It rained that day, and the umbrellas made for a gorgeous picture for the couple.

Photos You'd Like to Display

Whether you'll use them as table centerpieces or line up silver-framed portraits from all of your family weddings and favorite shots of you as a couple, photos add a lovely, personalized touch. Here is where you'll list the framed photos you want to bring in for décor, and organize getting others from relatives and friends to create a lineup of terrific portraits:

Picture	We Own It	Get It From	Returned

Additional Décor Items

___Lights

___Theme items

___Cultural items

___Pedestals for floral arrangements

___Framed oversized photo of bride and groom for
entryway

## 27

DJ or Band? Entertaining Your Crowd

You might already know whether you want a DJ or a band as your main entertainment for the reception. There are pros and cons to each—such as price package differences, hiring one person vs. hiring twelve and having to *feed* them as part of your catering bill. There are stylistic differences you may consider, such as the elegance of a twelve-piece orchestra vs. the hip, club-hopping environment provided by a great DJ. But first, think about which *other* kinds of musicians you might want for your cocktail hour or for other spotlight performances during your reception (and after-party!):

___Pianist

___Flutist

___Cellist

___Jazz band

___Ethnic musicians

___Harpist

___Trumpeter

___Guitarist (or guitarist duo)

___Singer(s)—soloist, a cappella group, Doo Wop

group, opera singers, etc.

___Others:

Breaking It Down

You might want to make your party a real show by having different performers for each segment of your celebration. So think about the following:

___Cocktail party (pianist or cellist)

___Dinner hour (pianist or guitarist)

___Dancing hours (DJ or band, jazz trio)

___Dessert hour (guitarist, flutist, pianist, DJ playing instrumental music)

___After-party (jazz trio, pianist)

___Morning-after breakfast (pianist, flutist)

___Other:

WHERE TO FIND MUSICIANS

You'll find great musicians, bands, and DJs through the usual channels of referrals, but you also could find the ideal performers at the most surprising of locations. Here's where to start your search and collect the business cards of experts you'll audition:

___Referrals from recently married friends and family.

___Expert referrals from your wedding coordinator and site managers. (They may have a concert pianist on staff!)

___Through a professional musician association. (Check out www.musicintheair.com if you're in the New York City area, and look for federations like these in your area.)

___Performances at bridal expos and showcases.

___Hotel lobbies. (Their pianists, harpists and cellists often work weddings as well.)

___Bookstores and cafes. (Guitarists and musicians often make extra money on the side by booking these appearances.)

___University performing arts departments or musical academies. (Your wedding would be great for a talented student's resume and portfolio!)

___Other (One bride found a terrific guitarist performing in a city park.):

SETTING UP AUDITIONS

Once you've narrowed down your list to possible experts who will play on your day, it's time to audition them. They'll come in, set up, and play for you the kinds of songs they'll perform on your wedding day, and you'll get to see them in action—not just for their talent, but for their sense of style and how they would interact with your crowd. Remember, DJs and band leaders can create a great atmosphere with their energy level, how they speak to your group, the way in which they take requests, and their general friendliness. So if that DJ seems to be a pompous, self-important jerk, cross him off your list.

SPECIAL SONGS TO BE PLAYED:

Here is where you'll record any special songs you'd definitely like played at your celebration:

Cocktail hour:

-
-
-
-
-

As the wedding party enters the room:
As bride and groom enter the room:
First dance song:
Father-daughter dance song:
Mother-son dance song:
Spotlight dances by request:

-
-
-
-
-

During the bouquet toss:
During the garter removal:
During the cake cutting:
As we make our exit:
Additional party songs we love:

-
-
-
-
-
-
-
-

- •
- •
- •
- •
- •
- •
- •

After-party play list:

- •
- •
- •
- •
- •

"Do Not Play!" List

You'd be wise to let your performers know that some songs are NOT to be played, such as your recently-divorced sister's wedding song (yikes!), any songs that remind you of your ex or old flames, or any songs your crowd would not appreciate:

- •
- •
- •
- •

FOR EACH MUSICIAN YOU HIRE:

Make sure you have a rock-solid contract with all details spelled out. Record when deposits and final payments are due, the exact hours they are to perform, and you can even write into your contract what you want them to wear (as in, tuxedos to match your crowd, all-black outfits, no sequin-studded jackets.)

28

Special Words

The words spoken on your wedding day last forever. Not just your vows, but the toasts proposed at
all of your wedding events. And we're not just talking about the Best Man's toast at the reception.
Anyone who loves you can toast you at any party. *You*
can toast your families, your wedding party, and
even each other at any time.

Before we get into who's toasting whom (and
when), check out the following qualities of a great
wedding toast:

- Sentimental
- Humorous
- Good-natured
- Personalized
- Very "You"
- Engaging
- Family-friendly
- Brief
- Inspiring
- Comfortable
- Smile-inducing
- Heartfelt
- Shows gratitude
- Shows insight into who you are, by sharing anecdotes

EVENTS WHERE TOASTS MAY BE PROPOSED

Start thinking now about the many events where you
or a loved one might ask everyone to lift their glasses
in tribute. You might use this list to start planning

the wording of your own toasts, with speeches tailored to each event, *or* ask special people in your life if they'd like to take the spotlight at a particular event:

__Engagement party

__The first planning meeting with the parents

__Your own first planning meeting, just the two of you

__A dinner or cocktail party with your wedding party

__Bridal showers

__Bridal brunches

__Post-shopping or post-fitting lunches with your bridesmaids or moms

__The bachelor party

__The bachelorette party

__Wedding weekend events

__The rehearsal dinner

__The morning-of-the-wedding breakfast or brunch

__The reception (of course!)

__The after-party

__The morning-after breakfast

__Other:

WHO DO YOU WANT TO TOAST

This is where you decide who *you* want to propose a thoughtful toast to, either on your own or together with your groom. And get double-use out of this checklist by highlighting or circling who you might ask to propose a special toast at the wedding—say, a memorial toast for your departed family members or friends.

___Both you and the groom can toast one another

___Bride's parents

___Bride's mother

___Bride's father

___Bride's stepparents

___Bride's grandparents

___Bride's most inspiring relatives (a favorite aunt and uncle who have been married for fifty years, etc.)

___Groom's parents

___Groom's mother

___Groom's father

___Groom's stepparents

___Groom's grandparents

___Groom's most inspiring relatives

___Your kids, if you have them

___Your Maid or Matron of Honor

___Your Best Man

___Your wedding party

___Your bridesmaids

___Your groomsmen

___The child attendants

___Special friends

___Guests who have traveled a great distance to attend the wedding

___The person or people who introduced the two of you to one another

___Your siblings

___Your godparents

___Your cousins

___Your work friends

___Anyone who helped you plan the wedding, or
   devoted extra time to helping you make favors
___Other:

SPECIAL TRIBUTES

Think about any special tributes that you'd like to
present at your wedding: a moment of silence for
departed relatives, the playing of your departed sister's favorite song, the lighting of a candle in memory of a departed friend, a toast to the Armed
Forces serving overseas.

Sentimental moments like this make a wedding
day all the richer, as you're paying tribute to those
in your hearts.

## 29

Wedding Favors and Gifts

Of course, the most important things your guests will take away from your wedding are unforgettable memories of how lovely you looked, what a beautiful ceremony you had, and what a fantastic party you threw. But they'll also take away a little something extra, something sweet, or long lasting to remind them of your day. Here are the top ideas for wedding favors; check off those you'll look into buying for your group:

___Chocolates
___Silver frames
___Silver bells
___Potted herbs
___Potted flowers
___Tree seedlings
___Frosted cookies
___Brownies
___Mints in tins
___Sugared almonds
___Chocolate coffee beans
___Single roses

___Charm bracelets
___Music (mix CDs)
___Quotation books
___Books of poetry
___Journals
___Sunglasses
___Scarves
___Magnets
___Mugs
___Pampering products
___Candles and holders
___Classic toys

__Fortune cookies	__Wine charms
__Cigars	__Statuettes/figurines
__Wine bottles	__Martini glass sets

Your own ideas:

-
-
-
-
-

Your chosen wedding favors are:
Website or store name:
needed:
Price:

FAVOR PRESENTATION

It's all in the presentation. You'll wrap, box, or label your favors in the following manner:

__Tulle pouch
__Clear acrylic box
__Gift box with silk flower on top
__Basket
__No wrapping
__Other:

Wrapping Source

Visit www.bayleysboxes.com for terrific, creative packaging ideas and ordering information.

Labels

A lovely personalized label affixed to your favors puts your stamp on them, reminding your guests of the terrific time they had at your wedding. Here, you'll design what you want your label to look like and read:

___We'll order our labels online

___We'll order from a catalog

___We'll order at a store

___We'll make them ourselves on our home computer using a graphics program

___No labels

___Other:

GIFTS FOR YOUR LOVED ONES AND WEDDING PARTY

These ideas on the previous pages might be your choices for gifts to your wedding party and parents, so consider those as well. Here, you'll consider ideas for gifts to your nearest and dearest:

For Parents:

___Gift certificate for a dinner out at a nice restaurant

___An engraved silver frame to hold your wedding portrait

___A fine bottle of champagne to toast you after your departure

___A bit of pampering after all their hard work

___A gift certificate to a spa for massages and "the works"

___A five-star brunch

___A music mix CD of the songs that remind you of great family moments

___A video or DVD compilation of your favorite family home movies

___Tickets to see a show, concert, or sports event

___Other:

For Your Maid of Honor and Bridesmaids:

___Silver heart lockets

___Silver heart bracelets

___Jewelry sets to wear on the wedding day—earrings, necklace, and bracelets

___Charm bracelets with fun theme charms

___Initial necklaces with diamond chips in them

___Satin robes and slippers

___Pampering baskets (www.bedbathandbeyond.com)

___Silver frames with photos of you all together

___Music mix CDs with all your favorite songs

___Bottles of fine wine

___Tickets to see a show or sports event

___A gift certificate to a spa for the works

___A gift certificate to a restaurant for dinner or brunch

___Other:

For Your Best Man and Groomsmen:

__Silver flasks

__Silver money clips

__Cufflinks for the wedding day

__Engraved beer mugs

__Fine cigars

__Bottles of fine brandy, port, or cognac

__Music mix CDs

__Tickets to see a show or sports event

__A gift certificate to a restaurant for dinner or brunch

__Other:

For the Child Attendants:

__Music boxes

__Charm bracelets

__A heart locket

__A much-wanted toy

__Personalized backpacks filled with toys

__Tickets to see a show or sports event

__Collectible

__Gift certificate to a toy store

__Gift certificate to a music store

__Gift certificate to a clothing store

__Other:

WHO ELSE GETS A GIFT?

What a gracious bride and groom you are when you give a thoughtful gift to other people playing a part in your wedding. Here is your potential gift recipient list:

___Your wedding coordinator

___Your grandparents

___People who let you use their house, car, or contacts to plan your wedding for less

___Your guest book attendant

___The people who performed readings or music for your ceremony

___Babysitters who watched the kids

___Any wedding experts who went above and beyond the call of duty

___Any neighbors who were *really* patient with all the noise late into the night from your after-party

___Others on your shopping list:

## 30

Your Rehearsal and Rehearsal Dinner

Everyone involved gathers at your invitation to the vitally important rehearsal session to learn the exact moves they are to make and when, at the wedding.

Let's cover the basics first...who is invited?

- Every member of the wedding party (and they may bring a guest of theirs)
- The child attendants and their parents
- Your parents
- Anyone who is performing a reading, music, or special ritual at the ceremony
- And of course, the officiant(s)

Now, who's running the show? Who will be in charge of lining everyone up, giving instructions, and basically "teaching" your collection of participants everything they need to know? Check your chosen ringleader here:

__The officiant

__The wedding coordinator

__The site manager

__You
__Other:

Line 'Em Up!

No matter who is running the show, it's up to you
to create the official lineup of your wedding party
members, instructing them on who will stand or
walk in what order. Create a list, filling in the
names of your groomsmen, and then your bridesmaids and others, in the order in which you prefer
them.

Stand or Walk?

__The men will stand waiting at the end of the aisle
__The men will walk in the processional

Groom is at the first position, the men are lined
up to his side in the following order:

Best Man:

Best Man:

Groomsman:

Groomsman:

Groomsman:

Groomsman:

Groomsman:

Groomsman:

The ring bearer will stand or sit next to:

The women's processional:

Bridesmaid:

Bridesmaid:

Bridesmaid:

Bridesmaid:

Bridesmaid:

Bridesmaid:

Bridesmaid:

Bridesmaid:

Maid of Honor:

Flower girl:

Flower girl:

The bride is escorted down the aisle and takes her place for the start of the ceremony.

Official Processional Rules

If you're marrying in a house of worship, your faith may prescribe its own traditional lineup of who walks in which order, who stands where, and how you all make your entrance. Ask your officiant, or check www.weddingchannel.com and other bridal websites for any religious rules on processionals.

Who will walk you down the aisle?

__Father

__Father and mother

__Father and stepfather

__Mother

__Stepfather

__Brother

__No one; you'll walk yourself down the aisle

___Other:

If your groom will be escorted to his position or walked down the aisle as well, it will be by:

___Father and mother

___Father

___Mother

___Other:

"Are We Ready to Begin?"

With the basics covered, it's now time for the officiant to lead you through the steps of the ceremony, including:

- Where to stand, sit, or kneel
- The opening statements, including any personalizations you request
- The official wedding ceremony words
- Readings
- Music
- Special tributes
- Ethnic or cultural rituals
- Your wedding vows
- The exchanging of your rings
- Your first kiss
- Your presentation as husband and wife
- The recessional

You may be asked to walk through the processional and recessional a few times, so that everyone knows their requirements entirely.

The rehearsal is not over at this point, though. Now it's time for you to ask the officiant, and encourage everyone in attendance to ask as well, any additional questions you might have. Some sample questions are:

- "Who lifts my veil to reveal my face, and when?"
- "Will you prompt us when it's time to sit or kneel, as some of our guests are not members of this church and may not know what to do?"
- "What do our non-Catholic wedding party members do when it's time to receive communion?"

List your important questions here:

-
-
-
-
-
-
-
-
-
-

SPECIAL INSTRUCTIONS

At this time, you'll give special instructions to the people who will perform various roles on the wedding day. Here are a few suggestions:

- Tell the Maid of Honor when, during your movements within the ceremony, she will have to adjust your train.
- Tell the ushers exactly how to escort guests to their seats, even suggesting some topics for wel-

come small talk, and remind them to walk slowly.

- Tell the guest book attendant where to stand with the book.
- Tell the people handing out the programs where they will stand and whether they give one program to each person, or one to each couple.
- Tell the person who will hand out the post ceremony toss-its when and how they should hand those tulle pouches out.
- Other:
- Other:
- Other:
- Other:
- Other:
- Other:

Here's where you record your wishes for your rehearsal dinner. Depending on who's planning it—whether your groom's parents have taken on the traditional role as the hosts of this party, or whether it's a total group effort between you all—the hosts will love knowing your preferences in order to make you happy.

Our Preferred Style:

__Formal, dress-up

__Formal, business dress

__Informal

__Super-casual

__At a restaurant or hotel ballroom

__At the hotel where the wedding will be held

__At parents' home

__At relative's home:

__At your home

__Outdoors, in a tent or at the beach

__At your favorite restaurant:

__At a winery

__Other:

Our Preferred Menu Style:

__Sit-down dinner, with pre-chosen meals served
   to guests

__Sit-down dinner, guests order off the menu

__Sit-down dinner, family-style

__Cocktail party only

__Cocktail hour followed by sit-down meal

__Buffet

__Dessert and champagne only

__Barbecue

__Clambake on the beach

__Other:

*Our Menu Wish List (i.e. Italian food, some vegetarian
options, Asian, Tex Mex, etc.):*

-
-
-
-

Our Guest List

You're in the know as far as who is participating in the wedding, so the rehearsal dinner hosts need to get the guest list from you. Remember to include the officiant and his or her guest as a classy and traditional move, and let the hosts know if you plan to invite any extra out-of-town guests to the rehearsal dinner as well.

-
-
-
-
-
-
-
-
-
-
-
-
-
-
-
-
-
-
-
-
-
-

-
-
-
-
-
-
-
-

Party Itinerary

- Mingling upon arrival.
- Host proposes the first toast.
- You toast your family, wedding party, and guests.
- Enjoy the meal and celebrations.
- Additional toasts ensue.
- Take plenty of pictures and video of this festive event—you can share prints later and post them on your wedding website.
- Give gifts to your wedding party, parents, kids, etc.
- Provide last-minute instructions, printed driving directions, and printed itineraries to your wedding party and families.
- Check that all wedding party members have everything they need in order for the big day.
- Close down the party after coffee and drinks, and then turn in early. You have a big day coming up!

Part Seven

Other Events

## 31

Wedding Day Beauty

Your beauty ritual doesn't just *start* on your wedding day. If you're like most brides-to-be, you schedule months' worth of beauty appointments way in advance. Like getting your hair cut and colored the appropriate three to four weeks before the big day, pre-tanning, getting your teeth whitened either at the dentists' office, or using eight weeks' worth of those whitening strips.

Here is where you'll keep track of all of your pre-wedding beauty appointments, perhaps even adding to the fun by taking a friend along or scheduling a lunch or coffee stop afterwards...

__Haircut

__Hair coloring

__Highlights

__Extensions

__Straightening

__Deep conditioner

__Scalp massage

__Practice hairstyle session before the wedding day

___Facial

___Electrolysis

___Facial waxing

___Eyebrow shaping

___Manicure

___Pedicure

___Acrylics

___Paraffin wax

___Tanning (spray-on or bed)

___Exfoliation

___Herbal/seaweed wraps

___Massages

___Aromatherapy sessions

___Other:

___Other:

YOUR WEDDING DAY BEAUTY PACKAGE

Here are just some of the things your spa or salon might offer with their bridal package:

- Rides to and from the spa/salon in a *limousine* for you and your maids
- Complimentary champagne in crystal flutes
- A catered breakfast in a private lounge just for you and your bridal party
- Catered hot hors d'oeuvres as you're getting ready
- Complimentary massage for you
- Complimentary foot massages for all of you
- Free digital photograph copies of your "before" and "after" pictures placed in a dual picture frame
- Free video of you all getting your hair and makeup

done, sharing a champagne toast—those conversations are captured on film for you forever!
- A free treatment for you (like your French manicure) when your four bridesmaids get their hair done at the same salon
- A free hairstyle for your flower girl when you and the bridesmaids get your hair done
- And more…

First, organize who gets to share the trip to the spa with you. List who gets to join you here:

Mothers:

Grandmothers:

Bridesmaids:

Flower girls:

Others:

Send in Invitations Early!

Be sure to mail or email each of these guests the complete wedding day beauty appointment schedule, so that everyone gets the royal treatment along with you that day! Lots of brides like to use Evite.com, so that they can see exactly who has RSVP'd. Then remind each guest at the rehearsal dinner before the wedding day!

GETTING READY AT HOME?

Don't want to go to a beauty salon or spa to get ready for your big day? Then you might either hire a professional stylist to come to your home and give you the royal treatment, or have a friend work her own magic with your hair and makeup.

## 32

Your Engagement Party

You may be the toast of *several* parties and celebrations as your wedding day approaches. You might even be in on the planning of several, such as wedding weekend events and even your rehearsal dinner. Here is where you'll record your plans, ideas, and guest lists for each of these events, perhaps giving much-appreciated guidance to the hosts.

Use this worksheet to share your preferences, or to make your own final plans, for the party:

Sample Ideas:

- An elegant, catered cocktail party at home.
- A classy dessert-and-champagne only affair at a hotel ballroom or at your home.
- A sit-down dinner at a five-star restaurant for your family and wedding party only.
- An afternoon cocktail party on the grounds of a winery.
- A family-style dinner at home, with all of your favorite family recipes on the menu.

Date:
Time:
Location:
Location website:
Site manager's name:
Site manager's contact info:

Theme or style:
Who's hosting this party:
Dress code:
RSVP date:

Invitation plans:

Invitation send-by date:

Décor:
-
-
-
-

Menu:
-
-
-
-
-
-
-
-

Cake or desserts:

-
-
-
-

Drinks:

-
-
-
-

Favors:

-
-

Activities/Games:

-
-
-
-

Rentals needed?

-
-
-

Notes:

Guest List

-
-
-
-
-
-
-
-
-
-
-
-
-
-
-
-
-
-
-
-
-
-
-
-
-
-
-
-
-
-
-
-
-
-
-
-
-
-
-

## 33

Your Bridal Shower

Use this worksheet to share your preferences, or to make your own final plans for the party:

Sample Ideas:

- An elegant catered buffet at a family member's or friend's home, with "Showers of Happiness" sheet cake for dessert.
- A catered buffet at a restaurant or hotel ballroom.
- A five-star brunch at a restaurant or hotel's elegant dining room.
- A lavish breakfast or afternoon tea at the home of a friend.
- A theme dinner event, such as an Asian night, a Mardi Gras party, an Oscars or Broadway theme party.
- A dessert-and-champagne soiree or cocktail party for your *coed* shower at a friend's or relative's home.

Date:
Time:
Location:

Location website:
Site manager's name:
Site manager's contact info:

Theme or style:
Who's hosting this party:
Dress code:
RSVP date:

Invitation plans:

Invitation send-by date:

Décor:

-
-
-
-

Menu:

-
-
-
-
-
-
-
-
-

Cake or desserts:

-

-
-
-

Drinks:

-

-

-

-

Favors:

-

-

Activities/Games:

-

-

-

-

Rentals needed?

-

-

-

Notes:

Guest List

-
-
-
-
-
-
-
-
-
-
-
-
-
-
-
-
-
-
-
-
-
-
-
-
-
-
-
-
-
-
-
-
-
-
-
-

## 34

Bridal Luncheons and Brunches

Use this worksheet to share your preferences, or to make your own final plans for the party:

Sample Ideas:

- Lunch out at a fabulous restaurant, eating *al fresco* on their garden terrace.
- An elegant brunch at a restaurant or hotel, with a lavish buffet spread, free champagne, and a pianist providing the mood music.
- Breakfast at home, with bagels and paninis—plus an assortment of fillings and toppings—on the do-it-yourself menu.
- Afternoon tea at a restaurant or hotel's well-appointed lobby.
- An excursion to a cultural restaurant, such as Thai food, Indian food, Mexican, Japanese, German, etc.

Date:

Time:

Location:

Location website:

Site manager's name:
Site manager's contact info:

Theme or style:
Who's hosting this party:
Dress code:
RSVP date:

Invitation plans:

Invitation send-by date:

Décor:

·

·

·

·

Menu:

·

·

·

·

·

·

·

·

·

Cake or desserts:

·

·

-
-

Drinks:

-
-
-
-

Favors:

-
-

Activities/Games:

-
-
-
-

Rentals needed?

-
-
-

Notes:

-
-
-
-
-
-
-
-
-
-
-
-
-
-
-
-
-
-
-
-
-
-
-
-
-
-
-
-
-
-
-
-
-
-
-
-

## 35

The Bachelor and Bachelorette Parties

Use this worksheet to share your preferences, or to make your own final plans, for the party:

Sample Ideas:

- Rent a limousine (or a party bus if there are more than twelve of you) and bar-hop to your heart's content—after starting off with a great dinner together.

- A coed party (so that no one wonders what the other is doing out on the town) at a restaurant, proceeding to a cigar bar or nightclub to dance the night away together.

- The new bachelorette party is decidedly less sleazy and more upscale...the girls all go to a spa for the weekend.

- Another coed party idea—get VIP box seats at a baseball game or football game, have the party catered or cook out at a tailgate party and then hit a lounge after the game.

- Everyone goes to Las Vegas for the weekend.

Date:

Time:

Location:

Location website:

Site Manager's name:

Site manager's contact info:

Theme or style:

Who's hosting this party:

Dress code:

RSVP date:

Invitation plans:

Invitation send-by date:

Décor:

-

-

-

-

Menu:

-

-

-

-

-

-

-

-

Cake or desserts:

-
-
-
-

Drinks:

-
-
-
-

Favors:

-
-

Activities/Games:

-
-
-
-

Rentals needed?

-
-
-

Notes:

Guest List

-
-
-
-
-
-
-
-
-
-
-
-
-
-
-
-
-
-
-
-
-
-
-
-
-
-
-
-
-
-
-
-
-
-
-
-
-

## 36

The After-Party

Use this worksheet to share your preferences, or to make your own final plans, for the party:

Sample Ideas:

- A relaxing cocktail party in the parents' hotel suite, with leftovers from the reception brought up to the room and enjoyed late-night.
- A trip to a nearby jazz club for cocktails and desserts.
- Take the leftover wine or champagne bottles out onto the beach (if you have a permit, of course) and await the sunrise.
- Proceed back to a friend's place for a midnight swim, dip in the hot tub, spontaneous barbecue, drinks, and snacks.
- Proceed to the hotel's lounge for drinks, snacks, and plenty of attention from other patrons.

Date:

Time:

Location:

Location website:

Site manager's name:
Site manager's contact info:

Theme or style:
Who's hosting this party:
Dress code:
RSVP date:

Invitation plans:

Invitation send-by date:

Décor:

-
-
-
-

Menu:

-
-
-
-
-
-
-
-
-

Cake or desserts:

-
-

-
-

Drinks:

-
-
-
-

Favors:

-
-

Activities/Games:

-
-
-
-

Rentals needed?

-
-
-

Notes:

Guest List

-
-
-
-
-
-
-
-
-
-
-
-
-
-
-
-
-
-
-
-
-
-
-
-
-
-
-
-
-
-
-
-
-
-
-
-
-
-

37

The Morning-After Breakfast

Use this worksheet to share your preferences, or to make your own final plans for the party:

Sample Ideas:

- Ala carte breakfast plan in a private dining room at the hotel.
- Sign up for the hotel's elegant brunch on Sunday morning, requesting a wing of the dining room to yourselves—free champagne, serving stations including a crepe or omelet bar, live entertainment, and an endless lineup of desserts makes this a crowd favorite.
- A catered or homemade breakfast buffet at home, served out on your terrace or out by the pool—ask a volunteer to man the waffle maker!
- An at-home collection of bagels and toppings, Krispy Kremes, and terrific coffee for everyone. Bloody Marys are on the menu for those with hangovers.
- A champagne breakfast using the fine china, an exclusive VIP guest list, and catered chafing dishes with gourmet breakfast choices like eggs

Benedict, crème brulee pancakes, and mimosa options.

Date:
Time:
Location:
Location website:
Site manager's name:
Site manager's contact info:

Theme or style:
Who's hosting this party:
Dress code:
RSVP date:

Invitation plans:

Invitation send-by date:

Décor:

•

•

•

•

Menu:

•

•

•

•

•

-
-
-
-

Cake or desserts:

-
-
-
-

Drinks

-
-
-
-

Favors:

-
-

Activities/Games:

-
-
-
-

Rentals needed?

-
-
-

Notes:

Guest List

-
-
-
-
-
-
-
-
-
-
-
-
-
-
-
-
-
-
-
-
-
-
-
-
-
-
-
-
-
-
-
-
-
-
-
-
-
-
-

38

Wedding Weekend Activities

A great wedding weekend provides plenty of activities—not just your wedding day—for those who see this event as their *vacation,* as well as a chance to catch up with family and friends they haven't seen in a while. So give them great choices of organized activities and lots of downtime they can fill on their own.

Mix Up Formality

Make sure you offer an equal mix of dress-up and casual events so that your guests can relax in jeans and sweaters at one event, then break out their dresses and heels (or suits) for another. Your choices could range the gamut between:

___Five-star formal   ___Family-style

___Semi-formal   ___Ultra-casual

___Formal

Dining Experiences:

___Your family's favorite restaurant

___A casual, family-style restaurant

___Dinner buffets

___Pizza night at the local pizzeria (or order-in)

__Backyard barbecue

__Clambake on the beach

__Family-style dinner at home

__Kid-friendly meals (if not outings to a costumed-character themed eatery)

__Brunches

__Breakfast out or at home

__Happy hour bar snacks at the local sports bar

__Fondue bar

__Dessert and champagne gathering at home or out

Cultural Meals:

__Sushi	__Portuguese	__Vegetarian
__Indian	__Spanish	__Vegan
__Thai	__Seafood	__Cajun
__Tapas	__Trendy	__Barbecue
__Mexican	fusion	__German
__Chinese	__Greek	__Other:
__Tuscan	__Italian	

Cultural Events:

__Movie theaters

__Stage shows

__Concerts (either paid at an arts center or free in the park)

__Museums

__Aquariums

__Historical tours

__House tours

___Haunted house tours

___Culinary tours

___Family farm outings (corn mazes, tractor rides, tours)

___Wineries

___Comedy clubs

___Outlet shopping trips (check www.outlet-bound.com)

___Antique shopping

___Bookstore trips (to see appearing authors and kids' favorite characters, such as at a story hour with activities)

___Other:

Active Outings:

___Tennis

___Golf

___Going to a sporting event

___Mini-golf

___Bowling

___Softball or touch-football game in the park

___Boating or kayaking

___Bike tour

___Group trip to the beach

___His side vs. her side tournament (softball, mini-golf, volleyball, etc.)

___Yard games: horseshoes, badminton, bocce, etc.

___Trip to the playground with the kids

___Wall climbing

___Other:

KNOW YOUR CROWD

Your college roommates are likely going to enjoy happy hours and softball tournaments way more than your grandparents will (unless you have *really* cool grandparents). So make sure you plan events that will suit your crowd and their tastes. Record your planned ideas here:

For Families with Kids:

-
-
-
-
-

For Singles:

-
-
-
-
-

For the Older Crowd:

-
-
-
-
-

For Non-Partiers:

-
-
-
-
-

For the Athletic:

-
-
-
-
-

For Serious Shoppers:

-
-
-
-
-

EVENT #1:

Now, use the planning forms that follow to sketch out your wishes for your chosen invitation-only activities. Make a separate copy for each event.

Date:

Time:

Location:

Location website:

Site manager's name:

Site manager's contact info:

the busy bride's essential wedding checklists

Theme or style:
Who's hosting this party:
Dress code:
RSVP date:

Invitation plans:

Invitation send-by date:

Décor:

-
-
-
-

Menu:

-
-
-
-
-
-
-
-
-

Cake or desserts:

-
-
-
-

Drinks:

-
-
-
-

Favors:

-

-

Activities/Games:

-

-

-

-

Rentals needed?

-

-

-

Notes:

Guest List

-
-
-
-
-
-
-
-
-
-
-
-
-
-
-
-
-
-
-
-
-
-
-
-
-
-
-
-
-
-
-
-
-
-
-
-
-
-
-
-
-
-

Use this worksheet to share your preferences, or to make your own final plans for the party:

Date:

Time:

Location:

Location website:

Site manager's name:

Site manager's contact info:

Theme or style:

Who's hosting this party:

Dress code:

RSVP date:

Invitation plans:

Invitation send-by date:

Décor:

-
-
-
-

Menu:

-
-
-
-

-
-
-
-
-

Cake or desserts:

-
-
-
-

Drinks:

-
-
-
-

Favors:

-
-

Activities/Games:

-
-
-
-

Rentals needed?

-
-
-

Notes:

Guest List

-
-
-
-
-
-
-
-
-
-
-
-
-
-
-
-
-
-
-
-
-
-
-
-
-
-
-
-
-
-
-
-
-
-
-
-

the busy bride's essential wedding checklists

Use this worksheet to share your preferences, or to make your own final plans for the party:

Date:

Time:

Location:

Location website:

Site manager's name:

Site manager's contact info:

Theme or style:

Who's hosting this party:

Dress code:

RSVP date:

Invitation plans:

Invitation send-by date:

Décor:

-
-
-
-

Menu:

-
-
-

-
-
-
-
-
-

Cake or desserts:

-
-
-
-

Drinks:

-
-
-
-

Favors:

-
-

Activities/Games:

-
-
-
-

Rentals needed?

-
-
-

Notes:

Guest List

-
-
-
-
-
-
-
-
-
-
-
-
-
-
-
-
-
-
-
-
-
-
-
-
-
-
-
-
-
-
-
-
-
-
-
-
-
-
-
-

Part Eight

After the Wedding

39

Saying Thank You

Throughout your own personal "wedding season," you've undoubtedly sent thank-you notes to guests who gave you shower and engagement gifts. Now, after the wedding, it's time to express your thanks to your guests and to all of the special people who helped your wedding come to life. That might be your parents who helped pay for the wedding, or your sister who saved the day by steaming the wrinkles out of your veil with fifteen minutes to go before the ceremony.

Now that the big event is over, you'll think back with a clear mind to really appreciate those who came through for you. Your gratitude can be expressed in so many ways:

___Sending a personal letter of thanks along with the printed official thank-you note

___Sending a beautiful bouquet of flowers

___Sending a gift certificate for dinner at a fabulous restaurant

___Sending a gift certificate to a five-star brunch

___Bringing a bottle of wine or champagne to their house when you visit after the wedding

___Getting them their own wedding photo album

___Having a gorgeous picture of *them* from your wedding enlarged and framed for display in their home

___Taking them out for dinner

___Cooking an amazing meal for them in your home

___Getting them tickets to a show or concert they've been dying to see

And most importantly...

___Being there for *them* in the future during their big life events and celebrations, giving your all, as they have done for you

___Maintaining your relationship with them in the future, keeping them as high priorities in your life

## 40

Name Change

If you wish to change (or hyphenate) your name after the wedding, you'll need to take some very necessary steps to make sure your identity is on the record. That means contacting everyone from the Social Security office to your gym to make sure they have your new name on file so that you exist by your current name.

This checklist helps you make sure that once you have *certified* copies of your marriage license to use as directed, you've put in your paperwork everywhere you need to:

Helpful Links

Visit www.weddingchannel.com and type in "name change" to find easy links right to the Social Security website and to your state's official website for name change registry information.

___Social Security
___Your driver's license (this can't be done online...you'll have to go the DMV in person)
___Your passport (this is done after your honeymoon)

___Your mortgage

___Your leases

___Your loans

___Your auto insurance

___Your health insurance

___Your will

___Your bank savings and checking accounts

___Your investment accounts

___Your employer

___Your credit card accounts

List Your Cards!

Make sure you get all of your credit card accounts changed. List each of your cards here:

-
-
-
-
-
-

___Your online accounts

___Your voter registration

___Any business associations you belong to

___Any personal clubs you belong to

___Your physicians

___Gym membership

___Yoga studio membership

___Rewards cards

___Your alumni association

___Magazine subscriptions
___The phone book
___Your phone account
___Your cell phone account
___Driver's club membership
___Neighborhood association membership
___All of your work colleagues, bosses, and contacts
___New business cards and letterhead
___All of your friends
___All of your family
___Others:

NOTE FROM THE AUTHOR

You're all set! Keep this checklist book handy at all times! Stay on top of filling in what you and your team have accomplished, highlight what still needs to be done, and personalize this book with your own unique tasks.

As time goes on, you'll enjoy a fabulous sense of accomplishment when you flip back over the many details you've handled like a pro, and you might just feel calmer and more in control of the process. There's a lot to do, but you're on it!

I wish you all the best of luck in your planning process and in your future together, and I invite you to send me your ideas and anecdotes for future editions of this book, and all of my other books in this series. You can reach me through my site, www.sharonnaylor.net.

Have a wonderful wedding!
All the best,

Sharon Naylor

Appendix #1

CREATE YOUR OWN CHECKLIST

Title:

___
___
___
___
___
___
___
___
___
___
___
___
___
___
___
___
___
___

Appendix #2

CREATE YOUR OWN CHECKLIST
Title:

Appendix #3

CREATE YOUR OWN CHART

Title:

Appendix #4

CREATE YOUR OWN CHART

Title:

Appendix #5

Name	Phone Number

Appendix #6

YOUR MASTER PHONE LIST

Name	Phone Number

Appendix #7

YOUR CRAFTS NOTES

Use this sheet to organize your shopping list, helpers list, and assembly plan for anything you plan to *make* for the wedding.

Index

A

B

C

D

E

F

G

P

R

S

About the Author

Sharon Naylor is the author of numerous books on weddings, including *Your Special Wedding Toasts*, *Your Special Wedding Vows*, *1000 Best Wedding Bargains*, and *1000 Best Secrets for Your Perfect Wedding* (Sourcebooks, 2004). She lives in Madison, New Jersey.